Good Food

Also by Tony Hodgson

Country People: An Endangered Species
SMH Books 2005
Pear Tree Cottage, Watersfield, Pulborough, West Sussex RH20 1NG

Good Food Stories

Our choices make the world of difference

TONY HODGSON

SHEPHEARD-WALWYN (PUBLISHERS) LTD

© Tony Hodgson 2006

All rights reserved. No part of this book may be
reproduced in any form without the written permission
of the publisher, Shepheard-Walwyn (Publishers) Ltd

First published in 2006 by
Shepheard-Walwyn (Publishers) Ltd
Suite 604, The Chandlery
50 Westminster Bridge Road
London SE1 7QY

British Library Cataloguing in Publication Data
A catalogue record of this book
is available from the British Library

ISBN-13: 978-0-85683-245-1
ISBN-10: 0-85683-245-6

Typeset by Alacrity,
Banwell Castle, Weston-super-Mare
Printed through Print Solutions, Wallington, Surrey

Contents

Introduction 7

I: Local

1	Independent Food Shops: Berwick-upon-Tweed	13
2	Farmers' Markets: Berwick and Nationwide	18
3	BOG: Borders Organic Gardeners	23
4	The Waltons and Borders Foundation for Rural Sustainability	29
5	BMR: Borders Machinery Ring	35
6	Local Food Works in Northern England	39
7	Selling Locally in the North East and South West of England	46

II: British and European

8	Community Land Trusts in Scotland and Elsewhere	55
9	A Co-operative in the East Midlands of England	60
10	Protecting Vulnerable Farmers in the Midi, France	64
11	Happy Hens in Gascony, France	70
12	Woodlands Farm, Lincolnshire	76
13	A Small Farm in the South West of England	82
14	The Green Patch in Northants: Community Supported Agriculture	88

III: Worldwide

15	Victorian Landcare in Australia	95
16	Manor Farm: Training Small Farmers in Kenya and East Africa	99
17	Comal: A Just Price in Honduras, Central America	104
18	Rural Links between India and Europe	109
19	Slow Food Spreading Out from Italy to the Rest of the World	115
20	What Can We Do?	119
	Appendix: Relevant Organisations	123
	Magazines and Newsletters	126

Introduction

THIS BOOK is a series of stories celebrating a tiny fraction of the courageous people who have set their face against the present trends in the food business. Two of the dominant features of these trends are the drift towards everything to do with food becoming bigger and more impersonal, and profits coming before concern for the needs of suppliers, customers, animals, plants and the soil on which we all depend.

First it is celebrating the delight to be found in tracking down local food. In the UK the call to 'eat the view' has been taken up in recent years in many different parts of the country. This is a call for people to buy the products of the earth which they can see from the kitchen if they live in the country or from the car if they are visitors. Farmers' Markets with their mileage limits, stalls like those run by the Women's Institute, restaurants like that at Wimpole Hall in Cambridgeshire, a National Trust property where food is grown on the home farm, and shops that specialise in selling local food are all part of this scene.

Next it is celebrating those who are protecting our soil, the plants that grow in it and the wild animals that depend on it. Landcare in Victoria, Australia, is an outstanding example of what can be done to bring back the quality of soil and in Southern Scotland the Borders Foundation for Rural Sustainability is based on a farm which combines a successful business with rich habitats for plants and therefore for birds and animals.

Then it examines how domestic animals can be given a fair deal. In the UK there have been vital steps forward in the last few years in concern for their welfare. But still much of the pork and poultry we consume has been reared in inhumane conditions and, because of the market, our dairy cows come under tremendous pressure. In a part of France it is being demonstrated that there need be no conflict between financial viability and providing poultry with an enjoyable existence. The people involved in this enterprise are the kind of medium-sized farmers who have been very vulnerable in the last fifty years. They have achieved their success not only by providing high quality goods but also by working together.

We need too to celebrate the small growers who up till recently have been the backbone of rural society. Support and training for smaller farmers and encouraging them to co-operate is an important way forward if we are ever to stop the present flight from the land. In this book we look at several examples of ways in which farmers can be supported, whether it is by a sympathetic union, a training college which puts itself within the range of the smallest farmer, or a ring which shares expertise and resources with large and small farmers alike.

Then there are the independent traders. We watch admiringly some of them at work in the UK and in the Third World and ask what qualities are needed not only for them to survive but to prosper in today's competitive world. All the businesses described in the book show exceptional enterprise and have high moral standards, not having to put profits for shareholders before everything else. In this context we can also celebrate the rediscovery of the age-old belief in the importance of a just price. Three of the enterprises we visit provide healthy food at a price which is fair both to producer and to consumer.

We look at ways in which people can regain control over the land in their own community, much of which was lost in England through the process of enclosure and in Scotland through the clearings. Particular progress is being made in Scotland where Community Land Trusts are enabling people to make decisions about the future use of the land where they live.

And perhaps one of the most important recoveries is that of traditional ways of cooking which belong to particular localities. The Slow Food Movement is nudging people back to using the old recipes and ingredients which belong in each place to put beside the vast array of cosmopolitan dishes now available to so many. It is also helping us to find enjoyment in giving each other space to sit down together and eat our home-cooked food at a reasonable pace.

A final development to celebrate is freedom of information. Until recently our relationship with the Third World has primarily been about passing on First World expertise to countries which need it. Gradually it is being discerned that there are many ways in which the boot might be on the other foot. When First World countries free themselves of their assumptions of superiority and are ready to listen to what the Third World has to teach them, miracles may occur. We see the germ of these happening in two First World producers who have applied the lessons they have learnt in the Third World. We also look at links of equality and friendship between people concerned about farming and the environment in Western Europe, ex-Communist countries and Asia. In this way we are being fair to what the Third World has to offer: this is globalisation working positively, as it can when it is not skewed in favour of the rich.

Local

∼ 1 ∼
Independent Food Shops
Berwick-upon-Tweed

IF YOU WALK into the Green Shop at any time of the day between 9am and 5.30pm from Monday to Saturday you will get a warm welcome. Ross or Pauline Boston, the proprietors, or one of their able assistants, will be there to greet you. You might find yourself signing a petition against GM crops, you might read about the latest events happening in the locality, you might take away a free copy of *Positive News*. And you will discover a wide range of wholesome foods and other goods. Ross and Pauline insist that everything in their shop is there for good ethical reasons. It is either fairly traded or locally produced or chemical free or allergen free or clear of unnecessary additives or energy efficient or recycled; if it is food it is bound to be organic.

There are over a thousand different pre-packaged items of organic foods to choose from, so most needs, certainly in the food department, can be catered for. And beside the packaged goods there is nearly always fresh bread available, and there is a supply of fresh organic fruit and vegetables with a growing local element. There is a wide range of excellent wines and beers costing very little more than equivalent non-organic brands. There is also a variety of cuts of meats. On the other hand eight out of ten of the foodstuffs are vegan and half are gluten-free.

The Green Shop has joined BAFTS, the British Association for Fair Trade Shops. This checks out all suppliers to make sure workers get a decent wage and live in good conditions. It also looks for disadvantaged groups, for instance women in societies where it is difficult for them to receive help in trading; it seeks out supplies from smallholdings, co-operatives and family-run group projects. BAFTS offers these people access to markets and use of marketing skills, research and development as well as financial security. It does this through guaranteed, negotiated, fixed prices and the availability of advances on the prices. BAFTS works through the Alternative Trading Organisations. These include such names as Traidcraft, People Tree, Shared Earth, Tearfund, Wonderworld and Pachamama. The Green Shop deals with a range of suppliers that cater especially for small shops such as Suma Foods, Green City, Infinity Foods and the Health Store. These are all wholesalers, but there are also producers whose food comes directly to the shop. One local organic gardener provides regular supplies of fresh herbs and a farm not too far away brings organic eggs and pies. Ross runs a personal delivery service to people's homes which is much appreciated.

Just to get a glimpse of the wide choice available, here are some of the cereals on sale. There are two kinds of organic cornflakes for those whose tastes are more traditional and there is also a cereal called Biobiz that looks very much like Weetabix. There is a good range of porridge oats, much of it milled locally and muesli base as well as the full muesli package from various sources. For children there are Koala Crisps and Gorilla Munchies, both coming with an environmental message.

And for those who want to be a little more adventurous there are Millet Rice, using a very nutritious grain that in this country is normally fed to birds, Heritage Flakes which contain spelt, quinoa and kanut, all grains that till recently had gone right out of fashion and Optimum Power with flaxseed, soy and blueberry. Unlike many of the mainstream cereals all these packages are low in salt and sugar and full of goodness.

The unique draw of the Green Shop is that it appeals to a very widespread desire to be more discriminating about shopping. Most of us cannot do all the research required to make sound decisions about all our purchases. But the Green Shop, like other similar shops, enables us to have confidence that what we buy will do the minimum of harm to ourselves, to other people and to the environment. We also can be sure that our purchasing power will be channeled into positive directions, whether it is helping struggling people in Third World countries or people having difficulty making a living in the Western economy.

Those who shop at the Green Shop are not only supporting something new, but they are also returning to ways that were tried and tested before the present rush to have cheap food from all over the globe. Although in the past there was far less food available, what was for sale had not been subjected to the barrage of chemicals found in so much of today's food. More and more people suspect that these pose health risks way beyond what we are officially told.

The Green Shop is set in Bridge Street, Berwick, a street specialising in independent small shops. There is an excellent privately owned bookshop, a photographic shop, a cookery shop, an old fashioned grocer and many others.

A few doors down from the Green Shop is the Market Shop with its own very distinctive flavour. One of the first impressions as you enter is the scent of a large selection of herbs. These are sold loose and can be bought in quantities as small as thirty grammes.

Jill Spence, who runs the shop, has two very important interrelated principles: she tries to respond whenever possible to what people want and she sees her work as the provision of a service, not primarily as a profit-making enterprise. She believes that good profits flow from good service.

Her trade is not confined to food and she has the reputation of having some of the most exciting and original cards in a town that is bursting with card shops. But she also has a wide selection of other goods bought as far as possible from ethical sources.

For fairly traded goods she shares with the Green Shop the supplier called Green City, but she has two distinctive sources in the Tree of Life which provides many of her supplements and Hider supplying British delicatessen foods like yoghurty raisins. Good health as well as good food is one of her watch words and she has a large number of homeopathic products by Weleda, one of the oldest names in the game. Another healthy product is Bioforce inspired by Jan de Vries the famous health guru. She, like Ross and Pauline, also caters for special diets by providing gluten free and dairy free goods. She recognises that young people like snacks, so to tempt them away from fast foods which have a high salt content she provides vegetable crisps and fruit leathers. She has also discovered that many older people are not yet sold on being organic, so she has inexpensive non-organic foods like dried fruit and porridge oats. On the other hand she also caters for needs which are not satisfied by the supermarkets, selling oriental specialities like curry bars, Kaffir lime leaves and fish sauce.

She has thought long and hard about such ticklish problems as the value of supplements and the need to eat organically. She believes that the real importance of supplements is to make up for the shortages to be found in our soil. One obvious example of this is selenium which has been progressively removed from the earth by decades of heavily industrialised agriculture. She also questions the ability of any food grown in this country to be purely organic, given the polluted environment by which we are all surrounded.

The Green Shop, with its insistence on all food being organic, and the Market Shop with its more flexible policies are the perfect foils for each other. Both attract their faithful followers, and plenty of casual visitors, as well as people who go to each shop for different purchases. Both are excellent examples of small, independent food shops that can flourish by having vision, determination and a willingness to go out of their way to bring a high standard of individual service to their customers.

Another very important factor is that most of the money spent in shops like the Green Shop and the Market Shop stays within the local economy. A family-run firm does what its name implies: it supports a local family as well as local people who work in the shop and others who supply a sizeable amount of the produce.

~ 2 ~
Farmers' Markets
Berwick and Nationwide

GRAHAM HEAD came to live in Northumberland in 1998. Born and brought up in Croydon, South London, where his father had always been a keen gardener, he moved from there to the outskirts of the city of Winchester in Hampshire. Here he started his passion for keeping middle white pigs with just two sows and a boar. With training in IT he was commuting back to London to work for high-powered city banks. He came North when he was headhunted by a prestigious Edinburgh company and searched the area till he found a place which had enough space to keep his pigs. He settled on a beautifully converted farm steading with a walled garden and a paddock making up an acre of land. On a three-hundred-foot ridge he has views to the North Sea and to the Kyloe and Cheviot hills.

After three years of combining the rearing of pigs with a full-time job in Edinburgh, he abandoned the city work and concentrated on bringing home the bacon. At this time a further two acres just up the lane became available: this was derelict land which had at one time been a small chicken farm and since then had been grazed by a horse. This enabled Graham to expand to twenty breeding sows and four boars. He was also extremely fortunate to locate a very able partner in Jacky McGuffie. Jacky had been born in Cumbria but spent his childhood in College Valley in the Cheviots only a few miles from Graham's patch. He had spent the previous twenty-five years looking after two thousand sheep in the Scottish Borders, just on the edge of the Lammermuir Hills in Berwickshire. He now lives in a village a few miles away from Graham where he trains sheepdogs and grows much of his own food. In Northumbrian dialect the word Guffie means 'pig' so his name is very appropriate.

So Graham and Jacky make an impressive pair. Graham has the business expertise to make this particular kind of small enterprise a success, and Jacky's experience of handling stock is second to few. Jacky comes in every weekday and takes care of all the routine feeding and cleaning jobs, while Graham sees to the marketing and distribution and the maintenance of a wide network of contacts. Once a week they spend a whole day together tackling all the jobs that require more than one pair of hands. The pigs spend much of their time being able to root in the luxurious grass; every so often fences have to be moved around to allow one patch of field to regenerate and another virgin space to be rooted up. Extra vigilance has to be shown at farrowing times as Graham does not believe in putting sows in crates, so there is always the possibility of one or two out of a litter of twelve piglets being crushed. The remaining piglets, which are not weaned till they are at least six weeks old, stay close to their mother till they are ready to fend for themselves: then they spend some more time in a secure shed being fed on pellets till they are old enough to go outside. Graham and Jacky mix a feed which consists of cereals, beans and peas only, with no growth promoters. Medicines are used only when required.

Graham's philosophy is that contented pigs make for contented customers because of the high quality of meat that results. Middle White pigs are so called because they were first produced by crossing large whites with small ones, now extinct. This took place at the end of the nineteenth century and in the first half of the twentieth they were very popular, but now they are a rare breed. Their meat is highly praised by well-known chefs – 'succulent', 'incredibly tender', 'with the crispiest skin' and 'best flavoured fat' – are some of their comments.

Graham believes that 'the new peasants', among whom he is proud to include himself, must differ from the old by specialising so that they can excel in one or two things rather than being all-rounders. His only diversification so far is to have a few 'clapped-out organic hens' so that he can have the pleasure of eating his own eggs and bacon for breakfast, and to begin to grow some of his own vegetables. So far he has been able to survive financially by sinking quite a lot of the capital he had built up through his previous earnings into the venture. He could go it alone and keep his head just above water that way, but as he can earn as much by a day's consultancy as by a month's pig-rearing, he may spend up to a month in a year returning to his old occupation. Thus he will be able to continue to employ both Jacky and a young couple who help him at weekends, releasing him to spend whole days at farmers' markets and similar events.

He also sees his work as a significant part of the local economy. He passes on his pigs to a neighbour with forty acres to finish them off. From there they may go to local butchers or to a flourishing farm shop close to Newcastle. Some of the meat Graham buys back and sells direct to local restaurants at farmers' markets and at food events. Another outlet is an up and coming small local chain called Reiver Foods.

When in 2001 there was talk of starting a farmers' market at his nearby town of Berwick-upon-Tweed Graham was the obvious person to spearhead the campaign. A previous attempt had failed, so there were a lot of negative vibes to overcome. As Graham was already a producer he was chosen to contact other producers who might be interested. He managed to find enough funding to cover a pilot trial of six months. After looking at five possible venues, the local arts theatre, the Maltings, was chosen. It combined the advantages of a large hall where stalls could he held under cover, however wet and windy it was outside, with a forecourt for the hardier souls. They started by hiring stalls from neighbouring markets, but this became prohibitively expensive, so half a dozen producers bought their own stalls and the rest used the tables provided inside. The pilot scheme went well and by half way through 2002 Graham and his colleagues had gathered together two dozen different suppliers.

As at all Farmers' Markets there is a restriction on the distance that food can travel and in this case it is fifty miles. The only exception is where a certain product range is not available within that strict limit. On a sunny day, quite common in Berwick, there are plenty of opportunities to enjoy the outside stalls, some with blue and white or red and white striped awnings giving a colourful welcome. There is always local fresh fish, mostly caught from the neighbouring ports of Seahouses and Eyemouth. Two farms have seasonal vegetables to offer, as well as flowers and jams and chutneys. Several of the stalls sell plants grown in local nurseries and a farm shop with its home-made cakes and jams is always there. When stalls bring out new products there is often an opportunity to try out the flavour: on one Sunday Graham Head was offering small pieces of his chorizo and a new flavour of sausage while another farm with a stall just inside the Maltings hall was tempting us to sample their salami. Other samples on offer included home-made chocolates, slices of cake, herb-flavoured olive oils, local cheeses, breads and chutney with nibbles. This tasting of samples is one of the ways in which conversations frequently spring up between the traders and their customers so that there is a constant buzz.

One of the effects of farmers' markets has been to draw producers, often traditional country people, out of their shells. Those who have helped to get the markets going have had to work together and make joint decisions and there is a friendly feeling of working towards a common cause. It has also helped customers to understand something of the concerns and needs of people who make their living from the land, as sometimes for the first time in their lives they come face to face with the people who are actually growing their food.

~ 3 ~
BOG
Borders Organic Gardeners

CHARBAGH is a Persian word meaning four gardens, a traditional way of dividing up the different forms of cultivation within an enclosed area. And Charbagh is the name of the home of David and Jayne Brettell, next to Lickar Moor Farm in North Northumberland. The Brettells arrived here in 2001, but five years before then they had started living in a farm worker's cottage with a long strip of garden in a neighbouring village.

David and Jayne were both brought up in the Home Counties of England where they had until the mid-nineties pursued their working lives, Jayne commuting into London and David spending fourteen years with the Metropolitan Police. Towards the end of that time he took a career break and spent three years travelling round the world.

Each of them was looking for a change of lifestyle and, as they had been committed vegetarians for twenty-five years, it was natural that they should look for somewhere to give them the time and space to grow their own vegetables. They found jobs which enabled them both to be flexible and to spend a fair amount of time working from home. Together they set up their own consultancy to help struggling community groups to move forward and to find the cash and expertise they needed.

During their first three years in the cottage they had gradually expanded the area they had to cultivate. They began by digging up their lawn to make a plot fifteen feet long and ten feet wide: they finished up by getting hold of a local allotment. But after that they decided to look around to find a place where they had plenty of room to develop all their dreams for a well-balanced plot. And so after a two-year search they alighted on Charbagh, the four gardens.

The spacious modern bungalow, with a tiny garden enclosed by a thick hedge and its acre of field, is in a beautiful, quiet spot facing away from its neighbour. This is a farmhouse and farm buildings serving a two hundred acre holding with beef cattle, a constant reminder of another way of eating. On this former field they set about developing at least four distinct patterns of land use. One of their first actions was to dig out a good-sized pond with a neighbouring bog patch which became full of kingcups. Then they planted hedges on the two sides of the field where there were none. On the side of the drive a row of copper beeches have been put in to form a screen both for beauty and protection. On the opposite side where the beef cattle graze they set a mixed hedge. At the end furthest from the house they left a rough patch to encourage wild life, and both there and in the little existing wood behind the house they have planted forty trees. Wetland and woods with wild life make up two of the ingredients of the garden and the third consists of an ornamental space with mown grass and borders with a good range of colour. And close to the house they have created the fourth element – the vegetable plot. With the help of a polytunnel David and

Jayne are working towards having an ample supply of vegetables at almost every season of the year. They believe that there is a natural rhythm to the way we eat vegetables: salads should be chiefly for the summer when cold food is most suitable, while root vegetables are particularly appropriate for cooking in the cold months. There are also vegetables which by early planting and storage can last all through the year. These include potatoes, stored in the bike shed, curly kale, a winter crop which goes on right through the seasons, and cauliflower and cabbages grown in and out of cover. Carrots and parsnips, stored in sand-filled tea chests, last for ten months of the year, as could onions and spinach. Tomatoes could last through the winter in the form of chutney or frozen in yoghurt pots, and other useful winter vegetables are leeks cropping from November to March, Brussels sprouts and purple sprouting broccoli. Both these latter were eaten by caterpillars during the summer but they then recovered to provide crops for human consumption. Allowing this to happen reflected a traditional philosophy which teaches that there is nothing wrong with sharing our food with other creatures, even if they are cabbage white butterflies, if we have abundance. The Brettells also encourage flowers to grow amongst the vegetables in order to attract more wild life and they leave the seeds on plants that have died for the same reason.

The polytunnel has also enabled the Brettells to grow crops which do not normally flourish in a Northern climate. This has included chillies, peppers, aubergines and sweetcorn. Other experimental crops include butter beans, mung beans and aduki beans which they planted in the polytunnel in May 2004, pushing at the boundaries of what our climate allows. Beans feature strongly in the diet: broad beans planted in October are ready in mid-May and then can be frozen to last the winter, and French beans planted in April are ready at the same time.

Neither Jayne nor David is fanatical about growing all their food, though one day they would love to be able to grow cereals and have them ground at the local watermill. So long as the food they buy is either local, organic or fairly traded, and preferably all three, they do from time to time add to their diet those things they are never likely to grow themselves.

David was brought up in a household where growing vegetables for home consumption was an important part of daily life, and so he was able to absorb from his father a delight in sitting down to a meal which included a fair quantity of food which had been picked an hour or so beforehand from the plot.

Although the Brettells' diet consists mainly of vegetables and cereals – Jayne says that these are the foods which help to keep her ying and yang in balance – there are times when even they cannot consume all the crops they produce. Then is the time for neighbours and friends to profit from their bounty.

They are also active members in the local organisation called Borders Organic Gardeners. This is believed to be the largest members' group of the national organic movement, the Henry Doubleday Research Association; its three hundred and fifty members stretch right along the Scottish Borders. The Brettells help to service the branch which lies on the south side of the border and to develop more interplay between the members in Northumberland. and at the time of writing David is chairing the organisation.

BOG has now been in existence for almost twenty years and its success has largely been due to a small band of dedicated people who have guided it faithfully through those years. One of the things that has held the group together is the magazine which comes out three times a year.

The Spring issues include the programme for the coming year. The first significant date is Potato Day, always held in early March. Scotland is famous for the quality of its seed potatoes and on this day gardeners gather to obtain their seed potatoes for the coming season. There is always a wide choice: this year there were eighty-two varieties and of these twenty-three were organic.

There are several visits. Here is the description of one in the Western Scottish Borders:

> … a neglected part-walled garden (one and a quarter acres) being replanted to supply locally grown fruit and veg, lots of soft fruit, apples and pears trained against a wall, raised beds with flowers and veg, one polytunnel up and another to be assembled ASAP. Beehives in use and hope to have hens by Spring. Pond and wildlife area. Plant propagation and tree nursery. Compost heaps and comfrey bed. Picnic Area.

Other garden visits include exchanges of seeds and plants. There are workshops and talks on such topics as willow harvesting and use, renovating plum and apple trees and building nest boxes for birds and homes for bats. These workshops and the informal conversations that go with them provide valuable opportunities for people to share their experiences. For beginners there is one called 'Getting Started'.

Towards the end of the year a vital diary date is Apple Day. A typical Apple Day lasts five hours and as well as the inevitable picnic there is identification of apples, tasting, tips and advice and displays. There is also a chance for members to buy and sell apples. Music and games are provided for the children. For BOG is not only about hard work: there is a lot of good fun and enjoyment, and for those who feel isolated and inadequate in their attempts to grow their own food there is tremendous support. BOG members vary from professionals who are growing food commercially to people who have a few vegetables in their back garden. All are driven by the desire to eat food which is healthy and, as far as is possible, seasonal, which has not travelled long distances and which tastes really good.

~ 4 ~
The Waltons
and Borders Foundation for Rural Sustainability

CHRIS AND DENISE Walton started their farming life with just eighty acres of land. This was the amount allocated for a network of smallholdings in the Scottish Borders parish of Mordington. These were some of many such settlements aimed at bringing back war veterans on to the land after the First World War. Although even in those days eighty acres was a comparatively small parcel of land, it has been shown again and again what enterprising things can be done with that kind of base. However the holders of those eighty acres were not given a free hand to do what they liked: there were very strict rules laid down by government about just how much cereal should be grown and how many cattle kept. All very praiseworthy in theory to ensure the maintenance of mixed farming, but it had the effect of curbing any budding entrepreneurs. These, if they went against the regulations, got booted out. So over the years most holdings were either amalgamated with others or abandoned to be consolidated into larger farms.

Chris and Denise have in fact followed this pattern, but in their case it has been to the immense benefit of the whole area. Their first move was to team up with their neighbours and to form a joint holding of two hundred and thirty acres: this included rough ground which belonged to the owners of the whole estate. The next partnership was with Amanda Cayley whose family owned the estate. She inherited the neighbouring farm of Peelham with its three hundred acres, so that brought the acreage up to over five hundred. By 2004 with the addition of some rented land the partners had the use of seven hundred acres in all.

You would have thought that was plenty to be going on with. But Chris and Denise reckon that in the present farming climate a thousand acres, the size of a 'small farm' in the USA, is rapidly becoming the minimum in this country for profitability without a particular speciality.

One of the specialities that these partners are going for is a landscape which is friendly to wildlife. They already have one large pond which is carefully managed to attract plants, animals and birds and they are planning to dig another. Although this does not bring in a great deal of money it does bring the approval of the RSPB which is monitoring their bird count three times a year. They are very pleased with the rise in number of two endangered species, tree sparrows and grey partridges. In both cases they started from scratch and the number of tree sparrows had risen to over fifty in quite a short time. They also have plenty of snipe, woodcock and merlin, all birds whose numbers have dropped elsewhere and they are delighted that the number of skylarks is increasing.

Within this landscape the Waltons keep their animals as extensively as possible: that means that they all have as much room as possible in which to move about. This includes the lambs and the cattle but some of the stars of the farm are the pigs which have a large enclosure surrounded by trees in which to roam, to root and to mate. These pigs produce outstandingly good bacon, sausages, pork chops and, the latest in the range, salamis: these are also sold in the local Farmers' Market along with the lamb and the beef.

Some years ago the Waltons decided not to go wholly organic so that they use a minimum of artificial fertilisers and pesticides. They therefore act as a good demonstration to other farms of how it is possible to combine real care for the countryside and concern for the welfare of all animals with conventional methods.

One of the factors in all this is the Waltons' choice of diversification. They have decided to make a cross country course for horses all round their land. Apart from bringing in cash this has the excellent spin-off of providing a wide buffer between arable fields: this gives the birds a generous corridor between the various patches of woodland.

The Waltons are very disappointed that the new grant system from Europe does not give sufficient encouragement to the planting of trees. If agricultural land is turned over to woodland, subsidy is lost unless the land was of such poor quality that it could not be used for anything else. They want to practise agroforestry, where stock are grazed under trees, but again they are thwarted by a regulation that states that if there are more than fifty trees on an acre there is no grant forthcoming. They are also sad that orchards have been left out of the grant system, which can only lead to the further grubbing up of fruit trees.

Their experience of wrestling with such regulations has helped them in their next major task. This is the creation of farm venture groups. They are conscious that the farming community has received such a battering from many different sources that there has been a loss of nerve among many. So they see their first job as restoring confidence in farming families, helping them to discover their skills and how they can best use them.

To bring this about they have started what they call kitchen table consultation. They gather together between six and ten people who may be drawn from as many as five different farms to find out first of all what skills they have between them. The group may include husbands, partners, wives, older children, other relatives and employees. In one group it was discovered that between them they had the ability to offer business management, engineering, wine-tasting, catering and being a nursery nurse as well as their farming expertise. After this skills audit is done the group is encouraged to do an ecological audit of their land to see what actual and potential possibilities there are for developing wild life friendly habitats. Groups are then encouraged to come up with ideas of ways in which they could diversify, making the best use of their skills and their land. One group is considering the possibility of starting a renewable energy scheme run on a community basis. Another group is looking at ways in which a local history project could be set up on their land. Two groups have already got started: one has set up a team to go to other farms and build log cabins to order for the use of visitors. The other one is also linked to tourism: their farms are positioned close to the dramatic cliff tops of St Abbs and they are taking visitors on rides in four wheel drive vehicles through breathtaking scenery. Although this does not sound particularly eco-friendly they have in fact signed up to a protocol which will ensure that there is no negative ecological effect.

One of the very valuable side effects of these venture groups is to bring farmers out of the isolation which has afflicted so much of the farming community. In the past resistance to co-operation with other farmers has been high, but in these desperate times for small farmers more and more are realising that they just must go into some kind of partnership with others in order to survive at all.

Another advantage has been that Chris and Denise have enabled farmers to share the burden of all the rules and regulations connected with diversifying. In one case a group had to contact no less than fourteen local authorities in order to obtain permission to do what they wanted to do. Such hassle is beyond the time constraints of one solitary farmer trying to make ends meet on their own.

Another tool which the Waltons have at their disposal is a logistics map. After the decision has been made to go ahead with a project the groups need to be helped to decide who does what, when and where. For instance there may be one person who is best qualified to deal with health and safety issues and to negotiate with the officer deputed to enforce them.

The Waltons have to keep a delicate balance between spoon-feeding groups and letting them make their own mistakes. The important thing is that the groups come up with the ideas themselves and then become progressively enthusiastic about seeing them through. Some groups need a great deal of nurturing in the initial stages, while others, once they have decided on their direction, can take off with only the minimum of help.

The drive behind the Waltons' initiatives is the belief that it is immensely important to keep people on the land without their having to go out of their farms to bring in the money. Every project which they encourage and which they engage in themselves is about using land to the best advantage, combined with healthy farming.

This accounts for the name of the their organisation – Borders Foundation for Rural Sustainability. The Waltons believe passionately that rural areas can again become sustainable if the talents and experience that are sometimes hidden within country people can be exposed and brought into full service.

~ 5 ~
BMR
Borders Machinery Ring

SEWAGE SLUDGE, shredded pallets, crab waste, paper pulp, straw and forest brush – what's left over when trees have been cut down – all these waste products are on line to become the fertiliser of the future.

An ambitious project is under way in the Scottish Borders to develop a new system of effectively composting all these locally generated wastes. It has the upbeat name of WIN – waste into nutrients – and the trials are being carried out by Borders Machinery Ring – BMR.

It is promising local landowners and farmers a whole raft of benefits: improved soils at minimum cost, new opportunities for contract work, effective composting sites for each farm, the provision of an alternative to peat for sale to gardeners and a way of cutting down on waste disposal in accordance with EU regulations.

BMR is just one of some thirty Machinery Rings scattered round Britain, but having started in 1987 it is one of the oldest. When it began it had just thirty-five members: now it has six hundred.

As their name implies Machinery Rings began with the aim of helping farmers obtain the machinery they needed for particular jobs without having to fork out vast sums on capital payments. Thus they have always been of particular value to small and medium farmers who need to keep their overheads down. One of the main reasons why so many small farms have gone out of business is that they have tried to go it alone, and in a world dominated by large corporations, this can be fatal.

Depending on the type of farming carried on in the local area Machinery Rings will try to cater for all the normal services which will be needed by providing both labour and equipment. In arable areas this will include such activities as cultivating, drilling, combining and straw baling. In areas where stock is being reared there will be hay and silage making, fencing, livestock services and slurry handling. In all areas there will be drainage, fertiliser spreading, property maintenance and farm record keeping.

But some Machinery Rings go way beyond the run of the mill requirements of a farm. BMR, for instance, lists among the services it can provide reflexology, knitwear, fishing, clay pigeon shooting, small woodland grant applications, child care, loo hire, bull service, water divining and water quality testing. Perhaps one of the most vital services, now that many local abattoirs have been closed, is that several machinery rings provide mobile slaughter and butchery services.

Machinery Rings can contribute to helping farmers look in new directions to bring in additional income. In tourist areas they can encourage farmers to have small caravan sites, they can assist with setting up trekking either on ponies or on motor bikes and they can help with the provision of holiday accommodation from unwanted buildings; in fruit growing areas they can help with such enterprises as pick your own.

Machinery Rings help to bridge the gulfs existing today between the big, medium and small scale growers, the organic and what is called in BMR's brochure 'normal' and the large and small supplier, for all of these can be fellow members. As well as pioneering organic compost Borders Machine Ring is happy to supply farms with agrochemicals and artificial fertiliser.

Machinery Rings also take the pain out of a lot of operations which small growers in particular may find difficult and/or risky. They will get quotations which are highly competitive from firms that can be relied on. This includes finding reliable tradesmen to do maintenance work, an invaluable service. They can negotiate deals and they can iron out any problems that may arise in the transactions. They can send in immediate help when a grower has been hit by bad weather, illness or mechanical breakdown; they can deal with invoices and sort out when the suppliers are to be paid. All these things can be headaches, if not disasters, if handled on a one-to-one basis, and Machinery Rings have the expertise to prevent things from going wrong at very little cost.

Machinery Rings have helped farmers to work together even more closely, forming what is now called umbrella farming. This can happen in at least two ways. Farmers can club together to take on a large contract, like straw baling, providing potatoes for stock feeding, hedge trimming for local authorities or grounds maintenance. Small individual farmers would find such projects difficult to sustain. Another way is for a group of farmers to pool their purchasing to reduce costs and they can also bring down costs by sharing both machinery and labour. Machinery Rings have brought into being what can really be called co-operatives.

If the strong can help the weak rather than just profiting from their misfortunes we shall begin to see a different spirit in farming from that which has prevailed in so many places over the last fifty years. Small farms, if they are given a chance, have an immense amount to teach larger ones, so that there can be a two way flow of inspiration and ideas as well as practical exchange.

~6~
Local Food Works
in Northern England

THERE IS A BUZZ at St Benedict's Church of England Church Centre at Cowpen, part of Blyth in Northumberland. Nine ladies, one gentleman and two small children are all waiting for the weekly Friday morning arrival of their bags of fresh fruit and vegetables. And while they wait they chat and tell stories and laugh. For some of them this is the best moment of the week. They are nearly all volunteers for the local food co-op and volunteering entitles you not only to have a chat but also you get a free bag of food. The job of the volunteers is to sort the boxes of fruit, vegetables and salad that come in from the main sorting office into bags. So a typical midsummer fruit bag will contain four apples, five bananas, two nectarines, four small oranges and a punnet of strawberries. The salad may include, as well as the inevitable lettuce, tomato and cucumber, a couple of peppers, some radishes and a small bunch of spring onions. For the vegetable bag there are carrots, onions, broccoli, cabbage and, as a special novelty, a corn on the cob: this comes complete with three recipes and a breakdown of the amount of fat, fibre, protein, carbohydrates and calories it adds to the diet. There are half bags for pensioners living on their own, and boxes of free-range Northumbrian eggs are also available.

All these foods come from local growers or they have been bought at the wholesale market in the Newcastle area at five o'clock in the morning by the administrator of the Co-op, Anthony. Anthony took on this job at the end of 2003 after twenty years of being a sub-postmaster. One of the reasons he left that work was that he found his new bosses were only interested in the financial profit being made by the post offices. They could not see the value of Anthony being there to listen to people and to be a focus for building community. For them the only thing that mattered was the amount of money changing hands.

So in his present post Anthony sees as one of the main values of his work the opportunity to bring people together and to give them dignity as well as better health. He is operating in some of the most deprived areas of the North East with high crime rates and low self-esteem. Despite this, two of the communities he serves have taken off well with an average of thirty to fifty bags per week. The other area besides Cowpen has the delightful name of Isabella. This group meets in the local community centre and Anthony has his eye on several other community centres in the area to provide future bases of operation. In Cowpen he has chosen not to use the community centre as it is already fully occupied with its own activities. On the day we visited this centre a young lady sitting in a wheelchair was busy sowing seeds inside a polytunnel. Jean, the dynamic manager, is creating a haven of beauty and refreshment for the local people and visitors. She has some allotments which she cannot develop at present, but it looks as though the local council is going to use them as a growing/training resource and Anthony hopes he may be able to market the produce.

Anthony has helped to secure sufficient funds from the Northern Rock Foundation to appoint another full-time worker to be alongside him for the next three years. This means he can now fulfil the role to which he was appointed – a rural food development officer. This will enable him to reach out in all sorts of ways: he wants to make contact with more local growers who could provide him with a steady supply of fruit and vegetables; he hopes to develop the four neighbouring communities in Seaton Valley, three of which have in the past been mining villages.

His work has attracted a great deal of interest from health professionals who recognise the improvements in health that flow from a better diet, and the Blyth Valley Health Trust has given funding to the project. He is also supported by Blyth Valley Community Matters which originally set up the Co-op with the Countryside Agency, and the Borough Council allows him to use premises rent free. Other useful contacts have been Surestart and local schools where he can give demonstrations on how to use fresh vegetables and fruit in the diet of both children and adults. He reckons his work fits in very well with several subjects in the national curriculum. One particularly successful example is the making of fruit smoothies.

One area, from which Anthony is steering clear at present, has its own independent greengrocer who is working hard to make a living. This man is also very community spirited and active in supporting local activities. But there are plenty of areas where at present people have to travel considerable distances to find a good source of fresh food. When they do find them, they may discover that the food co-ops on their doorstep represent better value.

Anthony's aim is to encourage more and more people to think seriously about what they are eating, how much of their present food is heavily processed and/or ready cooked and how a steady intake of fresh fruit, vegetables and eggs can radically improve their health. The work in Northumberland was inspired by developments three years earlier in neighbouring Cumbria.

In the year 2000 Sharron Rourke, a local business woman, was appointed the manager of a new initiative in her native county. It was called the Rural Regeneration Unit and it has now become a company in its own right. Sharron had previously been a nurse and so she was aware of the appalling effects that a bad diet was having on the health of many of the people in the poorer parts of Cumbria.

The Unit was set up by a partnership of the Countryside Alliance, the local Health Action Zone, the Borough Council and Mitchells, a livestock auctioneer. There were two main driving forces: the first was to see whether it was possible to find local sources of healthy food which were cheap enough for poorer people to be able to afford them. The second was to find good, steady markets for local producers.

People in large housing estates had to be persuaded of the need to change their eating habits in order to increase the amount of fresh food they ate, but growers also had to be convinced that such an enterprise had any chance of succeeding. It all began when six families agreed that they would put aside money from their weekly food budget to buy fresh vegetables even though they believed they could not afford it. Then Sharron found Tim, a local market gardener, who was willing to commit himself to supplying the required amount of vegetables every week for a trial period. The six families were so pleased with their bags of fresh produce that they told all their friends and soon the numbers grew.

Not long after this the Foot and Mouth Disease struck Cumbria and the urgency to find alternative incomes for farmers became heightened. Since that time Sharron has been working with two wholesalers who receive fresh food from local suppliers and pass it on to the co-op. She has also discovered another market gardener who has helped to keep supplies flowing, as well as the fertile garden of a local prison.

The forty food co-ops are managed by members who are volunteers. They will take the orders, collect the money and ring the suppliers to let them know how much is needed. For the fruit bags the rule is to have English apples and pears when they are in season and fairly traded citrus fruits and bananas from places which are free of conflict. Apart from fruit and vegetables some co-ops have access to bulk orders of meat, fish, cheeses and dried foods. For these goods the members specify what they want and how much they are prepared to pay – for instance they may order £1 worth of mince – and they pay in advance. They are given a number which matches the number on the coolbox containing their delivery. That box is then returned to the supplier for re-use. Those who are able are expected to come and collect their supplies, but deliveries are made to the homes of people who for any reason cannot do this. Both supplier and customer are getting good value for money. The suppliers have gained by having regular orders without any hassle and the customers have gained by being able to buy fresh food at prices well below what they would have to pay in most shops.

After four years of operation the Rural Regeneration Unit was supplying no less than eight thousand people with fresh food, and for many of those the intake of fresh food has doubled. The local health authorities have noticed the considerable improvement in health among those families as their diets have changed for the better.

The Unit has been reaching out into the community in other ways. As in Northumberland, one of the main targets has been the schools. Many of the primary schools have started patchwork gardens where children can grow their own vegetables and they have planted apple and pear trees to bring fresh fruit in the future. The Unit also had a scheme to give bags of tangerines to every school child so that there would be fresh fruit to eat over Christmas as well as all the usual fat-forming Christmas delicacies.

Sharron has arranged for local suppliers to deliver fruit to forty schools for them to sell in the tuck shop. This has been accompanied by health promotion talks and tasting sessions. The school pays the suppliers something in the region of 10p an item and then sells them on at cost. Some schools, with the agreement of parents, charge double and then put all the profits to paying for the children to have free trips out. Others encourage children to eat more fruit with the well-known slogan 'Buy one, get one free'.

The co-ops have affected their local communities in other ways as well. They have helped people who have been suffering from isolation, either in city or country, to socialise and to have a real purpose for meeting others. The average size of a co-op is between forty and fifty families, small enough for everyone who wishes to get to know everyone else. Some co-ops have organised trips for young people, set up local football teams and started bingo clubs for the elderly. Members learn to care for each other and if someone fails to turn up for the order they may receive a visit to make sure they are all right. Other groups have initiated training sessions, with the result that members have gained sufficient skills to find paid employment.

Another vital skill has been encouraged by the unit: Sharron, as well as being a nurse, has also been involved in catering, so she has set up classes in home cooking skills using fresh ingredients. She reported that one family, whose mother had learnt to boil potatoes, broccoli and carrots and then grate cheese on top, had given up their taste for chicken shapes and chips and demanded their mother's home cooking every day instead.

Food co-ops of this nature are not limited to Cumbria and Northumberland. Funding has been agreed by the Welsh Assembly to set up two pilot projects in Wales. So anywhere where there is poverty, openness to change and a local source of good fresh food, this kind of food co-op could be made to work.

~ 7 ~
Selling Locally
in the North East
and South West of England

FOXTONS is a popular wine bar at the centre of the small town of Berwick-upon-Tweed. On the wall of the dining room in large letters are these words: 'We are committed to using local fresh food whenever we can.' Then there is a list of some of their sources:

> Northumbria and Border Meats
> Berwick Shellfish
> Seahouses and Eyemouth fish
> Chain Bridge honey and mustards
> Doddington cheeses and ice cream
> Heatherslaw Mill cereals

This is one result of a campaign started by a local resident, Derek Sharman, which was called the Fresh Trading Initiative. This has persuaded local hotels, guest houses, restaurants and food shops to stock and serve local food whenever possible and to tell people about it.

In a survey Fresh Trading found that a remarkably high proportion of people, both visitors and residents, said Yes to this question: would they be influenced in their choice of where to eat and where to buy food by whether the food was being produced locally? The exact figures were nine out of ten for visitors and eight out of ten for residents, though this may well reflect aspiration more than reality.

Heatherslaw Mill is driven by a spectacular water mill. The building has been turned into a working museum and it is possible to view much of the process of grinding the corn. This turns into the delicious bread, cakes, biscuits and cereals which are to be found for sale throughout the district and beyond. You can eat them on the spot at the flourishing café attached to the mill. The mill is part of the attractive estate of Ford and Etal which markets itself as 'a great day out' with a miniature railway, a castle with historical connections to Flodden Field, two garden centres and a beautifully decorated village hall.

Another visitor attraction in the area is the Chain Bridge honey farm. Much of the farm's trade is from direct sales, as they have an amazing range of goods in some way connected with honey. These include lip balm, face and hand cream, beeswax furniture polish and candles, as well as many different kinds of honey.

Then there is Doddington Dairy. The result of diversification, Doddington Cheese is just one of a delightful range of local cheeses with names like Berwick Edge, Cuddy's Cave, named after St Cuthbert, and Reiver which adopts the name given to the local cross-border raiders of the past. Several of these local cheeses can be found at the four local butcher's shops owned by a Mr Foreman who lives in the nearby village of Norham, and because of the Fresh Trading Initiative you will also find them served at local restaurants and hotels. Doddington Dairy produces not only cheese, but also an extremely popular ice-cream which is also to be found throughout the area, with a variety of flavours including Newcastle Brown Ale.

Much of the fish eaten in North Northumberland is landed in the little Scottish port of Eyemouth, just across the border. Like all British fishing ports, Eyemouth has been hit by the results of the EC rules which have allowed so much overfishing. But it seems to have survived so far better than some, and though much of the catch is shipped off in refrigerated lorries to distant parts of the UK, a fair proportion finds its way into local mouths. There is also an important inshore fishing trade all along the coast and particularly on Holy Island: here local crab sandwiches are a very popular delicacy.

Another very successful local enterprise on Holy Island is St Aidan's Winery. A very high proportion of the crowds of visitors to Holy Island come away with bags which show that they have bought some Lindisfarne Mead. Also for sale are locally produced wines, kippers, shortbread and fudge, all of which make good sales.

These are all comparatively large enterprises which look beyond the local market. But there are also smaller concerns contributing significantly to the local economy. The Oxford Farm Shop near Berwick runs a very well-patronised restaurant serving meals in the holiday season right through the day till 7pm. You may sit in the conservatory eating your cakes and looking out at the extensive playground where children may enjoy themselves in freedom but under supervision. The farm shop makes its own jams and cakes which are to be found for sale in shops all over the district, and it has the dual advantages of being signposted off the A1 and of having a prestigious name.

All the outlets which subscribed to the Fresh Trading

Initiative benefited from the co-operative publicity and marketing which the Initiative provided. It marketed itself in a variety of ways: it organised high profile events to which it invited all its producer-members. There they were able both to advertise their wares and to sell direct. This role has been taken over by the Farmers' Markets. In fact the Initiative was largely responsible for creating the first successful Farmers' Market in the area after five years of delicate negotiations, and also took around a Road Show to demonstrate the delights of local food to more remote regions and to places where the concept of 'eating the view' had not yet become known. It has produced educational packs particularly for schools to counter the effects of 'Macdonaldisation' and it gave awards each year to those businesses that have excelled in providing local food for local people. It also started a food theme trail to enable both visitors and residents to hunt out as many as possible of the places where they can buy or consume local food.

Fortunately the Fresh Trading Initiative was by no means unique, nor did it work in isolation. Several of its members went to Herefordshire to learn about the exciting things happening in that county, and Taste of the West has been active all over the South West of England encouraging the purchase of local foods.

The small coastal town of Bridport in West Dorset has achieved Beacon status through its efforts to support local food. It recently received visitors from small towns in Australia, Ghana, Latvia and Poland, all wishing to discover how local food was successfully marketed in the area.

The enterprise behind the local food initiatives is called the West Dorset Food and Land Trust, and one of its most active hubs is the Washingpool Farm Shop.

Strategically placed only a couple of miles out of Bridport, this is the main outlet for a farm that has been growing high quality vegetables and soft fruit since the 1970s. The Eveleigh family started by selling some produce at the farm gate and after ten years they began trading in Bridport High Street. In the year 2000 they created their own purpose-built shop on the edge of their eighty-acre farm easily accessible to visitors. There is plenty of space for parking and plenty of space for displaying the wide variety of local products. Foremost among these are their own potatoes available most of the year and other seasonal vegetables and soft fruit which they have grown themselves. Thus in the Spring there are generally new carrots, gooseberries, spinach and herbs, while in the winter there are leeks, parsnips, curly kale and purple sprouting broccoli. But beside their own produce Washingpool Farm Shop's local produce embraces no less than forty other businesses.

If you are looking for dairy products there are three different makes of ice cream, three makers of local cheeses, and there is butter, organic milk, Jersey cream and yogurt. This represents the produce of nine different firms, mostly quite small.

For meat you can choose between Denhay bacon and sausages, Dorset Farms ham and bacon, Goodfellow's organically reared beef, Wallace's pork, venison and bison, Wyld Meadow lamb and Creedy's free-range chicken and duck. For those in search of fish there is Mere Fish Farm fresh and smoked trout, Flying Fish fishcakes and Wyndham's smoked fish.

For cereal products there are Moore's Dorset biscuits, Puddings and Pies which make cakes, tarts and quiches, Fudge's Bakery with sweet and savoury biscuits, Bridport pies and savouries, Evershot Bakery fresh bread and cakes, Tamarisk Farm organic flour and Dorset Cereals.

There are three sources of preserves, including jams, pickles, chutneys and mustards and Robert's makes sauces and salad dressings. Elwell Fruit Farm provides apples and pears and if the Washingpool range of vegetables does not meet all your requirements there are Riverfood organic vegetables, Sea Spring Farm chillies, peppers and tomatoes and a firm with the self-explanatory name of Olives et al.

That leaves you with Coastal free range eggs to pick up unless you are feeling like quails' eggs from Mrs Moss, local spring water from Spring Valley, chocolates from House of Dorchester, soup from the Dorset Blue Soup company, organic Clipper teas and coffees –the firm, not the product is local – and, if you want to organise a barbecue, locally fired Dorset charcoal.

So in one shop it is possible to obtain nearly all your food shopping needs and in the process support local businesses. And if you choose to consume some of them on the spot there is a café open every day from 10am to 4pm. Every autumn there is a food tasting event when customers can try out a whole range of different products.

Washingpool Farm demonstrates what can be done with just eighty acres of land. And the heartening thing is that three generations of Eveleighs have all been involved. John and Joyce started the horticulture business and then handed it over to the next generation, while the farm shop is managed by John's grandson who took a degree in agriculture and countryside management at the local agricultural college. John's grandson has his wife and parents working with him and there are also four people working on the horticulture side. So eighty acres and a shop can support eight workers and still make a handsome profit.

The Eveleigh family have an astonishing commitment to making local marketing work, but there is no reason why, given the will-power, the whole of rural UK could not return to becoming again a place where the majority of people choose to buy local, just because it is better for everyone.

II

British and European

~ 8 ~
Community Land Trusts
in Scotland and Elsewhere

GIGHA is an island in the Inner Hebrides, just three miles from the mainland coast of the Mull of Kintyre. It is five miles long and one wide and it has some of the best farming land in Argyll. But up till the year 2002 the land was owned by a long succession of individual lairds who often lived a long way from Gigha. Then the island went on the market for just over four million pounds and with the help of the Scottish Land Fund and the Highlands and Island Community Land Unit the islanders were able to buy it. So instead of one laird they had just under a hundred. But all the new owners lived and worked on the island and they had its future in their hearts. They have set up a Trust which manages all the financial affairs of the island. This has included raising a million pounds in two years to pay off the loan part of the money from the Scottish Land Fund. Now they are setting about finding the cash to do up the properties that have been allowed to fall into decay. They managed to ward off a bid by a developer who wanted to create an eighteen hole golf course and build fifty executive houses to go with it. Instead they are looking to a housing association to provide ten low-cost houses for people who want to live and work on the island. In 2004 a local resident built a new house: this was the first time such a thing had happened for seventeen years, for since the 1970s the population has halved. The Trust is also exploring the use of renewable energy, and craft units are being built beside the hotel. The future looks bright for the island to develop in a sustainable way, because for the first time in recent history the people of the community have control over their own land.

Gigha is just one example of the results of the Land Reform Bill passed by the Scottish Parliament to encourage crofters to buy their land from their landlords. Another equally successful buy-out was of the island of Eigg, the first whole Scottish island to be taken out of single ownership.

The idea of Community Land Trusts resurfaced in the USA towards the end of the twentieth century. In South Egremont, Massachusetts one of the first trusts owns twelve acres of land which it bought from a local family. A holding of just under ten acres is leased back to the original owner: he can enjoy the harvest of the apple trees which were planted by his grandfather. The remaining two and a half acres have become the site for four houses, each with the use of half an acre of land, and the E.F. Schumacher Library also with half an acre. Those who live in these houses own the building and can profit from any improvements they may make, but they do not own the land: when the house is sold the land remains with the Trust.

The Living Village Trust was formed in 1995 at Bishop's Castle in Shropshire. The village has two thousand inhabitants and like many villages in Britain it has been gentrified: local people have had to leave the village in search of work and cheaper housing. The Trust first bought an old pub: this it developed into a place where local businesses could have workspace. However it has allowed the pub to remain a pub with its own brewery on site; it won a CAMRA award for the best real ale in the county. Its next project was to buy an eighteen acre site, part of which it has used for affordable housing and the rest is for communal use, including both gardens and woodlands. One of the driving forces behind this enterprise is environmental awareness and all the houses have very high energy efficiency. Organic food production and recycling are also encouraged, and work is under way to create a combined heat and power company for sustainable energy throughout the village.

Also in England the Countryside Agency and Salford University are developing three pilot projects, one in Suffolk, one in North Lancashire and one on the Dorset/Somerset borders to test how Community Land Trusts can be adapted to quite different rural settings. In each case the driving force behind the Trust is also quite different. In Suffolk a powerful consortium has been formed to include Suffolk County Council, three housing associations, two district councils, two banks, the Prince's Trust and Small Business Service, along with interested individuals. In Lancashire the initiative began with a village appraisal in Slaidburn, which found the need not only for affordable housing but also for a Village Hall Centre and workspace for eleven businesses.

In Dorset and Somerset one of the prime movers has been the West Dorset Food and Land Trust mentioned in the last chapter. With the help of a Community Land Trust it is now working on obtaining land which could be made available especially to those who want to get into organic farming. At the same time it is developing an apprenticeship and training programme in association with existing organic growers and local colleges.

Community Land Trusts have been made possible by the wide range of finances which have become available. These have included European money, local regeneration funds, local charities, landowners, banks, building societies and housing associations with their access to housing corporation funding. There are also special government funding initiatives in rural areas following the BSE and Foot and Mouth crises.

Community Land Trusts are not just a new idea. They are a return to earlier ways when a large proportion of land in Britain was held by the community. Community Land Trusts are still to be found today dating back two centuries and more. One example is the village of Colton in Staffordshire which still holds sixty acres in trust and this is used exclusively by people living in three local villages. Similarly the Bournville Village Trust was developed by the Cadbury family for the benefit of people working in the local chocolate factory and it has maintained parkland as well as housing in a central part of Birmingham. The National Trust grew out of a Community Land Trust begun by Octavia Hill and John Ruskin in 1872 called St George's Fund. Its original objectives included the provision of affordable housing and the restoration of crafts and rural industries: the fact that only the third of its objectives, to maintain historic buildings and areas of natural beauty, was the only one that survived, is a historical accident.

Community Land Trusts, then, are looking back to those times when those who lived on property did not own it, but held it in return for services rendered to the community. In the same way modern CLTs tend to demand certain standards of ecological good practice in return for the use of the property. A CLT can provide an excellent balance between security and mobility. Farmers who wish to move on are assured of being able to receive a fair return for all the work they have put into the property, supposing the next generation does not want to go into farming. Unlike a tenant farmer the owner of a lease from a CLT will be able to walk away with the full value both of the building and the improvements that have been made. However the farmer may also pass on the lease to sons and daughters should they wish to take it on. If they do move on, this means that there is then opportunity for a new entrant to come in, rather than the land being swallowed up into a larger concern, while the farmhouse is sold off.

~ 9 ~
A Co-operative
in the East Midlands of England

IF YOU TRAVEL along the Bedford Road from the centre of Northampton you will find on your left a discreet but clear sign announcing The Daily Bread Co-operative.

This food co-op was set up back in the 1970s on the site of the old laundry of the nearby mental hospital. While maintaining many of its traditional features, the building has been transformed, but something of the caring tradition of the hospital remains. The co-operative makes a point of offering supportive work conditions to a certain number of people who are recovering from mental illness. This is just one of the features that makes this business operation a little bit different. Another is that ninety per cent of the full-time work force must be members of the co-operative, subscribing fully to all that it stands for. This leaves plenty of room for a wide spectrum of part-timers who fit their hours round their availability.

Another difference in the way the business is run is that the rate of pay varies not according to hierarchy but according to need: a single mother with five children is likely to receive considerably more than a husband whose wife is working, even if the job of the single mum is comparatively unskilled while the husband has a managerial post. There are therefore no fat cats and not even any shareholders: all profits from the co-operative are ploughed back into the business to make it more effective, or given away. Of that which is given away three quarters goes to developing countries to make up in a small way for the unfair terms of trade between the First and the Third World. The other quarter goes to local causes decided upon by the members of the co-operative.

Major decisions are made at the monthly meeting of all the members, while day to day decisions are taken either by the person in charge of that department or, if it is thought necessary, a memo is sent round to all the members for their assent. Decisions are arrived at by consensus and only once in the last six years has there had to be a vote on a major issue. This all takes time, but ultimately it is considered worthwhile to have everyone on board, rather than divided into warring camps. Once a week all the staff, including the part-timers, meet to review progress and to deal with any concerns that may have arisen, and less vital matters can also be dealt with at these sessions.

The atmosphere throughout the co-operative is one of unhurried but purposeful work in bright, clean and pleasant conditions. Much of the work behind the scenes consists of transferring the bulk supplies that arrive on the premises into manageable bites. One small room is given over entirely to herbs. In another larger room two people are packing fruits, nuts, sugar and flakes. There is no fancy packaging for any of the goods. Each large consignment is weighed out carefully and placed in plain glass jars or polythene bags with a standard Daily Bread label. This states the name of the product, the quantity, the ingredients if relevant, including any disclaimers, the date on which it was packed, the sell-by date and the name, address, telephone number and website of the co-operative. If the product is organic the label is green, if non-organic yellow – as simple as that, though the management expressed their concern that in five years' time there would be no such thing as real organic food if genetically modified crops were allowed to be grown commercially.

Some food is simply packed; some food which has already arrived packaged is divided up into appropriate bundles. Thus customers get the choice of buying a single item or getting a reduction by buying a tray full. Some food is actually made up on the premises: this includes flap jacks, fruit slices and one of their most popular lines, golden granola. This is a toasted breakfast cereal containing jumbo oats, honey, sunflower seeds, sunflower oil, raisin, hazelnuts, wheatgerm and sesame seeds. Honey, which also comes in bulk, is heated to just the right temperature to make it runny without destroying its enzymes. It is decanted into jars of various sizes and the larger jars, when returned, earn a 5p discount.

The criterion for stocking food is that it is nutritious. A high proportion of it, but not the majority, is organic. There are many fairly traded goods from overseas, but again not all foreign foods are fair trade. Hanging nonchalantly among the rows of foodstuffs there may be bags made by Tibetan refugees and sold at no profit to the co-operative. They would like to have more local produce and they were delighted that they had just found a good local source of organic potatoes.

By keeping all overheads to the minimum they aim to give fair prices both to the suppliers and the buyers.

A Co-operative

Certainly their formula seems to be working: in the week I visited their turnover had gone up twelve per cent in comparison with the equivalent week the previous year.

Daily Bread is an out of town shop, but it can easily be reached by bus from the town centre and there are two delivery vans which are in constant use. Deliveries are made within a fifty-mile radius and a Camphill Village Community is one of their regular dropping off points. Oxford, Coventry and Milton Keynes are among towns that are within easy reach and in some places one family will receive the orders for up to eleven others.

There is a comprehensive order list of products and orders can be sent by post, on the telephone, by email and now through the web. The product list gives a wealth of information including introductions to some of the staff, guidelines for healthy eating away from home and advice for parents on helping their children to eat healthily. Some of their leading suppliers advertise in this publication, thus helping to subsidise its production.

In all its operations Daily Bread is an interesting mix of realism and idealism. The manager explained to me that many such ventures had failed in the past because they were too idealistic. On the other hand, Daily Bread has certain very firm principles from which they do not deviate. These include keeping the price right, making the working conditions good, giving support to workers who need it, fair wages for all, good quality products and making the minimum of waste.

~ 10 ~
Protecting Vulnerable Farmers
in the Midi, France

MONTREDON is a farm in the Aveyron region of France on a high windy plateau north of Montpellier. When Jose Bove and his pregnant wife Alice first moved in, it had no mains water, no electricity and no telephone. It had been empty since the First World War.

Jose and Alice had met at Bordeaux University. Having completed their studies, they did three months' practical training in a farm in the Pyrenees. This farm took volunteers and showed them how to turn milk into cheese. Jose then applied to be registered as a conscientious objector; while he was waiting for a decision on this he spent a year on another farm learning how to make butter and yoghurt, while Alice worked on a local paper.

In Aveyron the farmers were opposing the extension of the local military base. This extension threatened the livelihoods of over a hundred of their number. Having learnt of their struggle, Jose and Alice, with the encouragement of the local farmers, moved into their new home in February 1976. They had just had their first child, a daughter called Helene. They were some of the first incomers to start working alongside the traditional farmers of the area. They won over the local population both by their competence as farmers and their dedication to the cause of fighting for their rights. After three years they had gained sufficient confidence in their farming skills to begin to make their own cheeses and sell them in the local markets. This was unheard of in those parts, as all milk went straight to Roquefort, to the major cheese factory there.

After eight years of struggle there was a change of government and President Mitterand agreed to the demands of the farmers. Over six thousand hectares were freed from the threat of occupation by the army and made available for farming. Jose and his companions worked out how the land could be rented from the State by a co-operative and shared out among the farmers. Each farmer took full possession of their portion of land, but after they left or died the land would go back to the co-operative. This made it possible for new people to come in and it served as a model for other experiments in co-operative ownership. The co-operative was able to lay down ground rules which, for instance, prevented overstocking and excessive use of nitrates.

While the struggle to keep the land was going on the farmers became more and more disillusioned with the local union and its associated young farmers' branch. In 1978 Alice and her young fellow-workers set up an alternative young farmers' union. Two important groups had already separated themselves from the mainstream farmers' union. One calling itself the Worker-Farmers had moved out of the union of their own accord; another group called Interpaysanne had been thrown out for being too radical in their demands. In 1981 these various movements came together to form Confederation Nationale des Syndicats de Travailleurs Paysans (CNSTP) with Jose as a leading member. At their first national conference in Paris that year they challenged the predominance of intensive farming. By 1990 the Confederation had achieved official recognition: its members were given a seat on some of the commissions on farming policy at both local and national level. This was an enormous step forward: up till then all official policy had been put together by the mainstream farmers' unions. These worked hand in glove both with the government and with Brussels. By 1995 the Confederation had won more than a quarter of the seats in the Chamber of Agriculture, giving it a substantial voice in farming policies.

In 1998 it published a charter for sustainable farming which had ten principles:

Principle 1 Production should be geared to enabling as many people as possible to go on working as farmers: the right to produce includes the right to work and the right to an income.

Principle 2 There should be solidarity with other farmers in Europe and in the rest of the world.

Principle 3 There must be respect for nature. Nature must be preserved to ensure the continuity of the use of the land by future generations.

Principle 4 We should make the most of abundant resources and protect those that are rare.

Principle 5 We must be transparent in our purchasing, production, processing and sale of agricultural produce.

Principle 6 Produce must be of good quality, taste good and be safe.

Principle 7 Farmers need to be able to make their own decisions about what they grow.

Principle 8 There should be partnership with others living in the countryside.

Principle 9 There should be a wide range of animals and plants on farms both for historic and economic reasons.

Principle 10 There is always a need to bear in mind the long-term and global context.

These principles underlie a belief that farming should be serving society by producing wholesome food, by halting the depopulation of the countryside and by giving priority to the environment in all farming activities. They are not so dogmatic that they rule out farmers who have not moved over to totally organic systems, but they define a new approach: this utterly rejects the progressive intensification of farming. They have provided a framework for the many farmers who are desperately unhappy with the way mainstream farming has gone. They often do not know how to break out of the treadmill of ever greater production per beast or per acre or per person regardless of the consequences.

Much of the resistance to intensive farming in France came from the treatment being meted out to calves. In 1980 there was a public outcry about the use of growth hormones in calf-breeding. People began to realise just how absurd was the current system. Calves were taken away from their mothers at the earliest possible moment; they were then fed milk which had been collected by lorry from the farm; this milk had gone to a factory where it was pasteurised, had its cream taken off, dried, reconstituted, packed and then returned to the specialist calf-breeder to feed the calf, thereby saving money!

Jose and his wife Alice had been influenced in their thinking by studying the work of Martin Luther King, of Cesar Chavez who championed the Latin American grapepickers in California and above all of Gandhi. In their own country they listened to the teaching of the great thinker, Jaques Ellul, who also advocated non-violent action. It was the example of such people that led Jose to perform one of the most striking non-violent actions carried out in Europe at the end of the twentieth century: he and a group of his friends dismantled a McDonalds. This had been erected in the town of Millau very close to the home of Roquefort cheese. The action rang a bell in the hearts of very many French people of all ages and all political and religious persuasions; they were increasingly horrified by the intrusion of junk food into a country which had prided itself on the quality and uniqueness of its own cuisine. When Jose was tried at Millau a hundred thousand people from all over France and beyond turned up to support him. The French government was so nervous of his appeal that they waited till after an election to imprison him, in case his entry into prison became a focus for political dissent.

Mainstream unions in nearly all European Union countries have been wedded to government policies which have been more or less dictated by the Common Agricultural Policy. Unions have not seen it as their role to protect the vulnerable members of the farming community, as the general consensus has been that they are disposable: their main thrust has been to protect the interests of the larger industrialised farms.

Is there any hope that this will change? As the emphasis gradually shifts from production to concern about the environment, animal welfare and food quality, there are signs of some movement: so it is just possible that the pioneering work of Jose Bove and his colleagues may have helped to pave the way for a change of heart throughout the European Union and beyond.

~11~
Happy Hens
in Gascony, France

MONSIEUR and Madame Casterède and their son Paul used to grow the usual selection of regional crops typical of Gers, the modern Department covering the ancient province of Gascony: some tobacco, some strawberries and some maize. They also reared ducks for cooking as well as for making the local speciality of foie gras. That was after nearly all the local vines had been ripped up because at that time Gascony wine was not a big seller. Madame Casterède's family had been living on the same plot of Gascon land for at least four generations, but it was becoming progressively harder to make ends meet and their young were losing interest.

Then in the year 2000 the Association Avicole du Gers came into the picture. If the Casterèdes were to put up a building for four thousand three hundred chickens the Association would provide them with all the birds, all the food and, most important, all the markets. All they had to do was to erect the fences to make sure the hens would not go astray and that they were safe from intruders, plant the trees under which they could shelter when they wished and look after their welfare. This last meant that they had to see that they were properly fed and watered, keep the deep litter in the sheds piling up and see that any birds that got pecked were removed and nursed back to health in the infirmary.

The Casterèdes eventually settled for four buildings and during the day the birds have the choice of staying inside with their mates, venturing outside into the flat space immediately next to the sheds or disappearing into the trees to peck and look for grubs. Their standard diet, which gradually flows into their feeding boxes, consists of a mixture of sorghum, maize, wheat and sunflower, all grown in France but not all organic. The birds live a minimum of eighty-one days before they are taken away to be slaughtered and during the course of that time each building uses up twenty-eight thousand kilos of food. Each day the birds in each building consume nine hundred litres of water which is always on tap.

After the eighty-one days the building is emptied, cleaned and disinfected and it must stay empty for at least three weeks. Because of these precautions there is a death rate of less than two per cent: hens that die have to be taken away to be examined, not buried on the farm. However the straw mixed with dung from the buildings may be used on the land for the Casterèdes' other growing activities: these include vegetables for their own use, and wheat and sunflowers for sale, the latter being one of the main cash crops of the area.

The Association Avicole du Gers brings together some five hundred small to medium farmers who, like the Casterèdes, accept the same very strict rules about the rearing of birds. One of the factors that encourages these very strict rules is that the people of Gers, like all traditional French people, are very particular about the food they eat. They believe that only birds which have been brought up in a caring and relaxed environment will taste really good. And so they are willing to support these locally grown products, even if they do cost a little more than frozen imported birds.

Apart from the yellow chickens in which the Casterèdes specialise, Gers also produces one fifth of the turkeys eaten at Christmas in France. They have had a happy life of at least one hundred and fifty days. The black farm turkeys of Gers are considered some of the finest in the country. Not far behind them are the grey chickens which reach the age of one hundred and five days minimum: these are the most long-lived of the French pullets reared for the table. The black and white birds, like the yellow ones, have a life of eighty-one days. One other time constraint is that all the birds must be consumed within nine days of their slaughter. Gers is fortunate to have access to three slaughter houses, one in the nearby town of Condom, so that birds do not have to be transported long distances to be slaughtered.

The Association Avicole represents an alternative route for mass production of food. Each unit is small enough to enable the farmers to have a personal care for their birds, but the total product is large enough to match the biggest industrial unit. In one year the Association produced no less than seven million pullets, one million guinea fowl, four hundred thousand turkeys and capons and thirty thousand geese.

The Association is not the only successful co-operative in the area. Gers is famous for at least three alcoholic drinks apart from its wine. Armagnac, a local alternative to Cognac, is produced only in Gers and from it there have sprung two other local drinks, a fortified wine called Floc and a liqueur called Pousse-Rapiere. The vinegrowers have come together to form a major co-operative for marketing these drinks nationwide, but there are also smaller co-operatives where a few local growers have clubbed together to sell their drinks to the local populace from their own premises. In the same manner the various farmers who produce melons and garlic have come together to market their wares.

Gers is special in Western Europe in that it still has a flourishing rural economy, being still untouched by some features of modern life: there are no motorways through the Department and no major industrial centre. Auch, the capital, which is also the largest town, has a population of only thirty thousand. Lectoure, one of the ancient centres, maintains its vigorous provincial life with just four thousand permanent inhabitants. Gers is also doing its best to resist attempts to industrialise agriculture: a recent plan to impose an intensive pig unit on the area provoked a storm of protest. There are a certain number of foreign residents and visitors but they have not yet crowded out the local culture.

The Casterèdes' farm is set in the community of Lamothe-Goas, not far from the town of Lectoure. It is a collection of hamlets with a total population of fifty-eight adults, but it boasts its own mayor and a lively newsletter: this deals with such subjects as the floral village competition, recycling, the closure of local small schools and the effect on farming of the extension of the European Community.

Every Friday the whole of Lectoure's long high street is turned into a bustling market with a great range of stalls. All traffic is kept out and the people are free to roam, browse and stand in groups to gossip with each other or with the market traders. There are always stalls selling poultry, both fresh and ready cooked. Some of the most succulent will come from the Association Avicole.

If you live in the vicinity of Lectoure you have four weekly markets to choose from, all on different days of the week. Tuesday is the turn of the neighbouring small medieval town of Fleurance. Fleurance market is larger and even more bustling than Lectoure and it takes over the whole of the centre of the town. Like Lectoure it is mainly a food market, though plants, clothes, jewellery and household goods also feature. Condom, a rather larger Cathedral town a few kilometres to the West, has one just as big on a Wednesday, centred on its own indoor market hall. On Thursdays the small fortified town of St Clar, one of the places known locally as bastides, has a market which specialises in selling the local garlics.

On a typical day in each of these markets there can be anything from ten to twenty stalls selling vegetables and fruit. Several of these have local, seasonal food grown by the people who are selling them. In the autumn for instance a smallholder would have on offer small strawberries which tasted just as strawberries always used to taste; he would have radishes with black skins and tender white insides; there would be oblong tomatoes with a rich flavour, sweet-tasting grapes, purple cauliflowers and the special mushroom of the region called cèpes. And in the early summer there would be cherries in abundance, peaches, apricots and melons, all grown in the area. But there are also honey stalls with a special by-product called royal jelly; it has this name because it is the food of the queen bee and good for the health. There are stalls selling a range of meat: locally made salamis, chorizos and sausages, and if you want some cuts of meat the man behind the stall is very happy to show off his skill in carving. There are wines and liqueurs to savour and all sorts of local cheeses mixed with those from other parts of France. There is always a whole stall dedicated to the local delicacy, pâté de foie gras. The influence of nearby Spain makes itself felt through a lady stirring a great pan of paella.

All these markets act as showpieces where organisations like the Association Avicole can make themselves known to residents and visitors alike. They are essential building blocks in the local rural economy along with the continued existence of smaller producers: these can make a profit through having both individual outlets and larger marketing facilities through co-operatives.

This pattern of production and marketing can act as a model for those rural areas which are looking for a more sustainable way forward. This can take the place of the concentration on large units of production, even larger middle men and multinational retail outlets which are becoming the norm in so many Western countries.

~ 12 ~
Woodlands Farm
Lincolnshire

ANDREW DENNIS is a fourth generation Lincolnshire farmer. His great grandfather, William, the son of a farm labourer, founded a dynasty which has established a unique reputation for successful farming. In 1996 Andrew made the dramatic decision to work towards converting the whole of his seventeen hundred acres to organic and caring agriculture.

The very first venture was to use some empty barns to house a flock of bronze turkeys. But they were not confined to the barns: spacious paddocks were provided in which they could range and trees were planted for shelter and roosting: it is often forgotten that turkeys are naturally woodland birds. Although there are now six hundred birds, each batch of young chicks is brought up separately, and when the time comes for slaughtering this is done discreetly out of the sight of others.

This humane treatment of animals is typical of the philosophy underlying Woodlands Farm today. Following the success of the turkeys Andrew launched into a veggie box scheme which has steadily grown to cover an area from Grimsby and Scunthorpe in the North to Northampton and Bedford in the South. This includes the whole of Lincolnshire, the whole of Rutland and parts of Leicestershire, Cambridgeshire, Northamptonshire and Bedfordshire. Although Andrew started locally he soon found that there was much more demand for his products outside his immediate locality of South Lincolnshire. He has set up thirteen collecting points where ten or more people come together to collect their boxes, but he also arranges deliveries to outlying homes. These boxes are of such high quality that they have been awarded the Veggie Box of the Year for the whole country. Two delightful touches are that the boxes are often graced by a flowering seasonal plant or a bunch of blooms and also each month they include a poem by the poet in residence, Clare Best.

Clare has been at Woodlands Farm since 2005, having received a grant from the Arts Council. She has run regular poetry workshops and competitions for local schoolchildren. These have had the dual effect of helping children to learn about organic farming and to express their learning in beautiful poems. Here is one of Clare's topical poems, very suitably about seed potatoes since the Dennis kingdom was founded on the extensive production of potatoes.

Seed Potatoes near the Wash

Slide the barn doors open, breathe in
the starchy musk of last year's swell,
listen to the vivid teeming silence …

Colleen, Orla, Desiree, Verity, Nicola,
racked through winter, floor to ceiling,
layer on layer of earthy stones.

Some days a milky northern sun
squints between roof and corrugated walls;
some nights, as black storms rush the fen,

> the keenest seeds open their eyes
> in grey electric light to chit and sprout
> for planting on a rising Easter tide.
>
> Clare Best*
Woodlands, 2006-07-01

Apart from her poems Clare makes very pertinent observations about what is going on around her. This one seems to sum up much of what organic farming is all about:

> We were walking with the plough and I was looking up at the gulls. I've always been very moved by the sight and sounds of gulls behind a plough. Andrew explained to me that, before the field was converted, when the soil had been poisoned for years by pesticides, there had been no birds following the plough because the soil was virtually dead – there were no worms. Now, since conversion, the soil was healthy again, the worms had come back and so had the birds.

For those of us who wonder why organic products are more expensive than conventional ones Andrew has three answers: first there is the period of conversion which must last at least two years and during which it is difficult to sell any produce from the land. Then with no artificial fertilisers production per acre may be as little as half that on conventional farms. and thirdly organic farming is much more labour intensive with such jobs as hand hoeing taking the place of spraying of herbicides by machine.

Andrew has found that one of the best places for recruiting keen and reliable workers is Poland. He is farming in an area which has gained an unfortunate notoriety for its treatment of workers from Eastern

---

* 'Seed Potatoes near the Wash' is reproduced here by kind permission of the author, Clare Best.

Europe. But Andrew is no gangmaster. The Poles in his employment have become valued members of his extended family and he has made frequent visits to Poland to visit them and their families. In 2006, when Piotr had been working with Andrew for three years, he got married in Poland. Here is an account by Andrew of the wedding feast:

> I discovered there was no shortage of delicious Polish dishes: *brszcz* (a clear beetroot soup), *rosol* (mouth-watering chicken broth made with leeks, carrots and parsnips), *sledz* (herrings), and best of all *bigos*, a popular Polish dish made with cabbage, dried mushrooms, tomatoes and *podgrzybki* (fatty pork pieces)... All those dishes: I'm struck by the realisation that people in the west rarely sit down together and eat traditional slow-cooked food unless it's a special occasion. This does not seem to apply so much in Eastern Europe where there appears to be a stronger sense of family and where time and emphasis is freely given to preparation of local, unprocessed food.

This is a quotation from one of Andrew's monthly newsletters, one of the means by which he holds together his large body of customers, workers and ex-workers. Here are some other comments on Polish agriculture:

> Polish apples are world famous. Numerous varieties were on display in shops and roadside stalls. I've also seen extensive orchards of pears and cherries.

Here is the description of an encounter he had with a Polish producer living close to Warsaw who has helped to foster the prosperity of small organic farms in Poland:

> Krystyna does not run a large operation. Farms in Poland are rarely more than around 20 acres. Together with her son, a horticultural graduate, she runs a small, highly-efficient market garden on which is produced a multitude

of crops mainly for hotels and ecological shops in Warsaw, as well as for her own Box scheme home delivery service. 'See this, Andrew,' she said, looking lovingly at the soil (and then at the compost heap) 'Believe me, before, not fertile. Now she will grow anything. It's a marriage, like a soup.' At which point a yellowhammer flew over.

On the down-side he comments:

> Today most of the vast state farms run by the communists have been closed. I've noticed huge abandoned farmyards and large areas of fertile land lying fallow. The farm staff have been laid off and without welfare payments they are destitute ... The government, meanwhile, is selling off the state farms to foreign investors, mostly German or Dutch. This at least provides much needed employment. And yet I sense a feeling of ambivalence. For some country people it is frustrating to see the land appropriated by other nations.

Andrew sees the Polish people as equal partners from whom we in England can learn much if we cease to regard them as people just to be exploited for cheap labour or feared as rivals in the sphere of organic growing.

Back home some of Andrew's most important contacts come through the farmers' markets in his area. Like the collection points for his veggie box scheme there are thirteen which bring in a good return of anything from one hundred and fifty pounds on a day to six hundred. But he cannot get to all of them, so in 2006 he was relying heavily on another member of his Polish family, Michal, who after eighteen months in the UK could speak good enough English to develop a rapport with the customers. Besides selling produce Andrew and Michal use the farmers' markets as recruiting-grounds for the veggie box scheme and on average they can pick up a an extra three customers in a day.

Although Woodlands Farm is not a small enterprise Andrew is determined to maintain a family atmosphere in the whole operation. One way he does this is to ensure that each sector has a distinctive entity. The packing of the veggie boxes from Monday to Thursday is carried out by a team of twelve young people working well together. Then there is a team looking after the Lincoln red cattle, others concerned with the organic lambs, the turkey flock and a department which deals with wholesale supplies to larger outlets. Customers are encouraged to come and visit on open days and to drop in at other times as well, and there is the steady outflow of recipes, poems, and newsletters to keep people in touch.

Andrew plugs into the wider organic movement in the UK through his links with the Soil Association, the Henry Doubleday Research Association and the Tastes of Lincolnshire of which he is a founder member. The success of his enterprise demonstrates how far the organic movement has been able to travel from the time when it was written off as something reserved for idealistic cranks, but also how it is possible to move on at this pace without losing one's soul in the process. And through his links with Eastern Europe and in particular with Poland Andrew has been able to grasp the wider context in which the British organic movement is set.

~ 13 ~
A Small Farm
in the South West of England

PETER AND MAGGIE Whiteman settled in mid-Devon in the middle of the nineteen eighties, and ever since they have made their living from just twenty-two acres of land. Up till then Peter had spent most of his adult life working in Africa and Asia. He was trained as a botanist and during those years abroad he learned to apply his knowledge of plants to the practical matters of growing them successfully. He did this in dry areas like Botswana, in mountainous areas like Kenya, Northern Pakistan and Nepal and in places that were both dry and mountainous like Ethiopia. He had discovered that if he was going to be of any use to the farmers among whom he was working he had to learn to listen as much as to teach.

One of the things he learnt from his travels was the importance of using to the full every resource that was available on the land he was working. This philosophy he applied when he settled down with Maggie at Lower Turley Farm. One of the skills Peter had picked up along the way was an ability to make delightful things from wood, and he was married to a wife who could do delightful things with felt.

A Small Farm

For most of Peter's needs there was no shortage of suitable wood. One of the pieces he has made from his own resources has been a fine rocking chair for his wife. He has also fashioned a ladder back chair with a seat of interwoven elm bark: it is said that this seat will last almost for ever. In the dining room there is a beautiful round table: this was made largely from an oak tree in his grounds. Peter had seasoned the wood himself and he put it together without using glue, nails or screws: the only exception was the table top which had to be screwed down to prevent it from buckling in the heat. On his land he has another oak tree which is coming to the end of its life and this should provide him with enough oak to last him for the next ten years.

One of Peter's great loves is making bows. One bow takes a week to make but it can be sold for two or three hundred pounds. Traditionally it has been believed that crossbows were always made from yew wood and there was no yew on the property. However a recent find in Denmark revealed a very old bow made from elm wood, so Peter decided that he too could make a fine bow from the elm tree on his own land. One bow he has made is lined with cowhide taken from one of his own cows.

One other vital wood ingredient is coppiced willow: Peter planted a stand of willow trees and he has used the branches to construct the sides of yurts: this is a kind of tent used commonly in such places as Turkmenistan. The construction of these yurts involves the use of three wood products of the property – willow branches for the sides, oak for the door and doorposts, and elm for the roof. The sides are so made that they can be concertinaed to fit onto a Bactrian camel and then stretched to form an ark to go round the circular space of the yurt.

Another equally vital local product for the yurt is the felt for its inner cladding. This comes from Peter and Maggie's sheep, specially bred to produce the finest possible wool for making into felts. And the main destination of this felt is Maggie's workshop. This is generally full of felt products which can be bought on the farm but which she takes round to local events. At one Glastonbury festival she managed to sell sixty items, including four Gandulf hats, and took orders for several more. Hats are her main forte but she also produces beautiful shawls and meticulously made shoes, the uppers of which are made from felt.

These uses of wood and felt were just two of the ways that the Whitemans managed to add value to the products of their little holding. When they first kept sheep they tried their hand at milking them and produced some delicious smoked cheese: this they sold in the local market. But that was knocked on the head by EU regulations; these required them to transport their six cheeses in a refrigerated van instead of a refrigerated ice box.

But there are plenty of other strings to their bows. A one-acre field is devoted to agroforestry: this has been planted with trees that not only produce wood but provide other by-products as well. There are perry pear trees, cider apple trees, a walnut tree and cherry trees. And below the trees the felt-producing sheep graze happily, thus preventing the need to keep down the undergrowth. One or two of the trees have suffered from having some of their bark stripped, but most have survived quite satisfactorily.

Another field is full of clover, with a mixture of other herbs. The clover seeds are spread on the ground along with the muck and produce a wonderfully prolific crop.

This is much appreciated by the three generations of cows, as is the beautifully sweet-smelling hay stored in the barn. Despite Devon's reputation for incessant rain the Whitemans have avoided resorting to silage with all its attendant pollution problems.

One of the most important features of the farm is the polytunnel. This has a variety of uses. Its warm climate is ideal for overwintering the sheep: after shearing their pelts can be hung up to dry alongside the vine, the tomatoes and the sweet potatoes, all of which are enjoying the fertility left by the sheep. There is a drip-feed irrigation system which dries up in August, making the cherry tomatoes taste even sweeter.

Up till recently Peter was supplying thirty boxes of vegetables on a year-round basis to local people who could come in, sign the book, pay their money and take their box. This provided a good steady income, as well as supplying thirty households with healthy organic food. Peter is now slowing this down, and the acre of garden has been reduced to a quarter of its former size. In this way, as he nears retirement, he can gradually move into subsistence farming, satisfying the needs of his own household. This includes a teenage daughter who, when she is not doing her school-work, helps out with the many jobs to be done round the place.

But like everything else on the farm that quarter acre is used to the full. There is a careful system of inter-planting, with plants that have spreading roots and upright stalks next to those that spread above ground and go straight down below. Also plants that are due to be harvested at different times of the year are allowed to rub shoulders. In this way the Whitemans achieve maximum productivity from their comparatively small plot.

Peter and Maggie have some of the characteristics of the peasant: they live simply but well. Much of their food comes from their own resources. They have very low inputs: neither of their two tractors, one of them a very old Fergie, would feature in the ads of the latest *Farmer's Weekly*. They do not yearn for foreign holidays – Peter does not go jetting off to the exotic places where he worked; he carries with him a storehouse of memories and lessons from those years. In sixteen years they have managed to get two separate weeks off when a trusted friend has looked after the place, but they are content with the beautiful spot where they are. Their three children have been educated locally at non-fee-paying schools.

Not everyone can make immaculate medieval cross bows or elegant and highly serviceable furniture. But everyone who has wood on their property can think of ways to make the most of that asset, whether it is by coppicing, by making planks or just selling firewood. And everyone who has land can plant trees, as the Whitemans have done, that yield profitable crops – there is great demand in the shops these days for such crops as organic hazel nuts or cherries.

Not everyone can make wonderful felt creations, as Maggie does, but anyone who has sheep can think of ways to add value to that asset and if, as happened to the Whitemans, EC regulations block one avenue, they can look for another. And for those who are concerned about frosts investment in a polytunnel pays for itself many times over, even if it is not put to so many uses as the Whitemans have found.

Lower Turley Farm also contradicts the myth that in the developed world small farms are non-viable unless their owners have another occupation off the farm. In terms of energy use and land use Lower Turley Farm is highly efficient, as there is very little energy used on the farm apart from human energy, and yet almost every square yard of the twenty-two acres contributes abundantly to its productivity. This surely is one powerful model for a type of farming for the future, combining maximum production with minimum input.

Although Peter and Maggie spend so much of their time on their farm, they are by no means alone: they are part of a vibrant association called Land Heritage. This small land-owning charity operates mainly in the South West of England. Here it brings together a network of people committed to encouraging 'systems of farming that build fertility, protect biodiversity and provide a sustainable supply of healthy food', as their publicity leaflet proclaims. Land Heritage lets out small farms to organic growers and it promotes the values of organic food. It has now brought these two things together by purchasing a demonstration farm where people can view the latest developments in organic farming at first hand.

~ 14 ~
The Green Patch
in Northants: Community Supported Agriculture

WHEN DAVID Sanders returned to his native Kettering in the late nineteen nineties he had worked in Belize in Latin America, in Senegal in West Africa and in India and Hong Kong in Asia. He came back full of ideas he had picked up from working alongside a rich variety of people from the Third World. He and his Chinese wife Bing Law were keen to help to create something of the sense of community which they had experienced in these countries. Although David's training was as a heating and ventilation engineer, his passion for a long time has been for organic and ecofriendly growing.

On coming to Northamptonshire they looked around to see what land was available: what was immediately available was a block of twenty-one former allotments overgrown with brambles up to five metres high and suffering from continuous acts of vandalism. As soon as they got hold of the land they quickly built up a team of local people from some of the most deprived parts of the town to get the place in order. This required hacking down the jungle, an experience familiar to David from his days in Latin America, and getting rid of all the accumulated rubbish.

They looked and are still looking for funding for the project, though they have high hopes of making it self-sufficient. They are great believers in partnerships and they teamed up with a local exchange trading system, a credit union and a community centre for young people to win a much coveted Single Regeneration Budget award. This, along with several other funds, has enabled them to develop the work on a sound financial footing. They now employ one other full-time worker apart from David himself. He is called Lee and he has a background in gamekeeping, but he turns his hand to all the practical jobs connected with the ever-expanding project. He is particularly involved in helping develop the move towards keeping more animals. Bees, free-range hens, fish and rare breeds of cattle are either already in place or in the pipeline.

This last promises to be a great help with one of the main emphases of the project, which is to work with children and young people. Already three local primary schools visit the place regularly and a part of the hectare of cultivated land is given over to raised beds which are managed by local children. Children chose the name The Green Patch and designed a special logo which is used all over the place, including on the project's van, about their only form of advertising. They are also working with several local schools to improve the quality of the children's food. They have even enlisted the help of Age Concern to send pensioners into schools to talk about healthy eating: one went in dressed as a banana.

Other partners in their work include those caring for mental patients in hospital, and Entry to Employment working with vulnerable young people: they both bring their clients to help on the place. They are fortunate in having the wholehearted support of the local council. Part of the reason for this is that the council can point to it as the one example of an environmentally friendly development which is also doing much for the building up a sense of community in an area which is otherwise quite neglected.

Much thought has been given to creating an environment which encourages wild life. Already thirty species of birds have been seen visiting the spot as well as frogs and newts in the small pond ; there are fox holes and they have even had a visit from a grass snake. Not bad in their semi-urban setting. They are encouraging the spread of marigolds to increase the number of pollinating insects, as well as wild flowers, grasses and sedges. There is also a sensory garden to help blind people appreciate the flora and next to it is a soft fruit patch. One hundred years ago this place was an orchard, so fruit trees are being planted all round the vegetable patch. This will help to restore a heritage which in many places is in danger of being lost. The next development is a nursery for shrubs and plants to sell so as to broaden their economic base.

The mainstay of the organisation is the provision of veggie boxes. Though most of the contents come from their own land they also supplement them with produce from an organic farm in Lincolnshire which is appropriately called Eden Farms. The produce is organic but the prices are kept to rock-bottom, sometimes cheaper than supermarkets and half the price of some other veggie box schemes. This is because many of the members just cannot afford to pay over the odds. The low prices are made possible by keeping the overheads to the minimum – noone connected with the project is going to get rich. David himself, though full-time, receives only a very small wage, while his wife, who does much of the book-keeping, works on a voluntary basis. Nearly all the work on the place is done by volunteers; some of them receive free food in return for their work and in this way they fulfil the terms of a growing new movement called Community Supported Agriculture or CSA.

CSA started in Japan where they called it Takei, meaning 'food with the farmers' face on it'. It is based on the twin ideas that many town-dwellers would like access to land without the responsibility of having a plot of their own and many growers can benefit from having extra hands, especially at busy times. Put these two together and you have production supported by the local community. This gives people a stake in the land who otherwise would not have it and it also acts as an enormous encouragement to struggling growers.

~III~
Worldwide

~15~
Victorian Landcare
in Australia

HARRY AND LYN Croll bought their one-hundred-and-forty-two-acre farm in Victoria, Australia, thirty years ago. The land was so degraded that it could only support twenty head of cattle. It was virtually a desert, with the water disappearing down a steep slope and flooding the surrounding area. The Crolls introduced a simple but effective system of irrigation. This consisted of a large dam and drainage using the natural contours of the land.

As the quality of the land has improved they have gradually increased the number of their cattle from twenty to one hundred and fifty. These cattle have achieved top quality status entirely naturally and the Crolls put it down to the copper, boron and other minerals in the many springs in the property. The Crolls' farm has become a haven for wild life including frogs, turtles, eels, swans, ducks, coots, egrets and cockatoos. When Lyn Croll was convalescing from two strokes, she spent much time in the company of a swan which was hatching her eggs: the cygnets adopted her as their foster mother.

Harry Croll calls himself a tray-a-day planter of trees. That means that he can plant around fifty trees a day, nearly all native species. For this to work, several areas have had to be fenced off to protect the saplings. He has received practical and financial help for this enterprise from the Bunyip Catchment Landcare Project Committee of Management, part of a state wide organisation called Landcare. Landcare is helping farmers all over Victoria to take better care of their land.

One of the features of Landcare has been its inclusiveness. It has managed to attract generous financial support from the federal and state governments, regional authorities and local councils. It has also been supported by businesses: these include Alcoa, the aluminium company, and fertiliser companies, despite the fact that it runs courses in organic farming. Its membership includes large landowners and small farmers – one of its top awards went to a couple living and working on a steep and difficult property of only eighty-seven acres (minute by Australian standards). It has enlisted the help of a whole range of volunteers: retired people, schoolchildren, overseas students, urban communities, the unemployed, business people, scouts and even tourists. In one area ninety-two indigenous people have been employed in vital conservation work and in another area a power station has been encouraged to plant two hundred thousand trees as a carbon sink. Students have put forward plans for regeneration of the land which have been taken on board by the local watcher-catchment authorities. A local newspaper has agreed to run a campaign on how to eradicate noxious weeds. A good balance has been kept in the gender structure of the training teams run by Landcare: in this traditionally male-dominated society young women have been encouraged to come forward with bright ideas for the future development of farming and care of the land.

One of the main planks of Landcare has been the provision of top class training at very reasonable prices. All sorts of practical skills have been passed on: these have included the ability to establish perennial pastures to increase soil moisture, retention and active management of native vegetation, integrated pest management and matching the right ways of bringing about fertility to particular pastures. But there is also training in management issues, like drawing up a whole farm plan, setting priorities, reporting on projects achieved and understanding grant applications.

One of the keys to the success of the project has been the provision of subsidies to make it worthwhile for farmers and landowners to invest in tree planting and in natural revegetation: one farmer received nearly all the two thousand Australian dollars required for a major fencing project. Another inbuilt advantage in the area is that there is a bank in Victoria called the Rural Finance Corporation which is specifically geared to the needs of farmers, with offices right across the state. It gives farmers the opportunity to have personal meetings with financial advisors who are experts in agriculture and it has a range of competitive, flexible lending packages specifically designed for farmers.

Landcare also looks to the future, having formed Junior Landcare. Not only are children deeply involved in programmes of conservation and tree planting but they also learn to put across the message of Landcare. For instance a group of young people from two schools joined together to put on a performance of singing, acting and dancing. They took as their theme the importance of an endangered species of bird called a White-Browed Tree Creeper which was losing its habitat. It has become an important part of the thinking of many rural schools in

Victoria to prepare children for farming in a way that looks after the land.

Like many parts of the world, Victoria still has a very long way to go before it becomes a rural paradise. Two hundred years of exploitation of the soil and neglect of the environmental consequences have taken their toll. But nonetheless there are considerable achievements. It is heartening that in at least one First World country erosion is now seen as a major problem that needs to be firmly tackled: and tackled, not by meddlesome bureaucrats or activists far removed from the land, but by the farmers and their families themselves.

~ 16 ~
Manor Farm
Training Small Farmers in Kenya and East Africa

TWO HUNDRED and fifty miles from Kenya's capital, Nairobi, lies the town of Kitale; and a few miles from the town lies Manor House Agricultural Centre. MHAC, as it is known, started life as a European farm called Manor Farm. In the fifties it was converted into a preparatory school largely for the children of European farmers. This came to an end in 1974 and the place lay derelict for some years.

Patrick Peacey, one of the teachers at the school, was given the vision to purchase the property for a new purpose. In 1981 he met a young American woman in Kenya who agreed to find the money necessary to buy it.

And so the Centre was born, a Trust being established three years later and substantial support coming from another American source. This was Ecology Action, based in California and developing ways of growing more and more food on less and less land. This came about through a combination of Chinese, French and Latin American farming techniques.

From the very start Patrick made sure that the management of the Centre was in the hands of Africans and that it targeted the particular needs of small farmers. The methods of farming taught at the school have a variety of names, but conservation farming is perhaps the easiest to grasp. This kind of farming is low cost and low impact. It encourages natural pest controls, deep soil preparation, crop rotation, composting, companion planting with close spacing of crops, and conservation of water and energy.

MHAC has managed to influence no less than seventy thousand farmers in fifteen thousand communities all over Kenya: it has also reached people in neighbouring countries, including Uganda, Tanzania, the Sudan and Zimbabwe – it has even spread its influence to Canada.

So how has this come about? MHAC has been running three kinds of courses. There are the one-week workshops which have been attended by farmer groups. There are three-month courses for people who can then go on to train others in the work. There are also two-year courses: these have equipped graduates to spread the message to the rest of the nation and beyond.

Although costs are kept to the minimum and many courses are sponsored by a variety of bodies, not all potential candidates can afford to travel to Kitale. MHAC is now busy setting up centres in other parts of Kenya to cater specifically for local people. Students on the two-year courses can use these centres as placements both to broaden their experience and to bring encouragement and new ideas to the students.

MHAC is a great believer in partnership and these are just some of the bodies with which they are working: Community Mobilisation against Desertification, Practical Action (till recently ITDG), the Anglican and Lutheran Churches in Kenya, Kenya Sustainable Agriculture and the Community Development Programme. It also receives support from the government: this comes through the Agriculture and Rural Development Extension department and the Soil and Water Conservation branch of the Ministry.

MHAC is looking closely at the subjects taught in the agricultural colleges: these are largely irrelevant to the needs of smaller farmers, as they advocate high input farming which is beyond the reach of all but the richest farmers. MHAC sees this as outdated teaching. As in many countries, there is a loss of enthusiasm for this kind of farming and some agricultural colleges are having to close down or to change to non-farming subjects. Like so many developing countries, Kenya embraced the so-called Green Revolution. This produced high yields only by the use of mechanisation and intensive use of pesticides and chemical fertilisers. MHAC sees this as one of the main causes of soil degradation.

Like many of his peers Simon Mwaura dropped out of school after finishing his primary education. He then went to Nairobi, where his brother found him a job in a hotel, a job which turned out to be a nightmare. So he returned to his home town of Thika jobless and broke. All he could find there was casual work which was irregular and uncertain, and in his frustration he turned to crime. However, before the law caught up with him, he decided to go into farming. He was encouraged in this by an MHAC graduate called Samuel Kangethe Mukuna. Samuel taught Simon about conservation farming and Simon started using green manures on his quarter acre plot of kale. He managed to dig a tube well, so he had a regular source of water and in the dry season his vegetables found an easy market. Simon enjoys having control over his life, dividing his time as he wishes between selling his produce, working on his plot and resting. He is determined never to lose these essential freedoms and to remain a farmer for the rest of his life. Meanwhile the majority of his friends who said they hated farming spend their time sitting around in the town or engaging in petty crime. However Simon's success impressed some of them and they gathered round him when MHAC people made a visit to his plot.

Another farmer called Bernard Mareithi owns two and a half acres in an area where most farmers reckon they need much larger acreages to make a living. Bernard has filled his small farm with trees that go well with crops and he is growing bananas, avocados, mangoes, paw paws and passion fruit, all using conservation farming techniques. From his small plot he has managed to satisfy all his needs, both for food and for income, as well as creating a beautiful and eco-friendly environment.

Patrick Kokiti has thirty double-dug vegetable plots on just one fifth of an acre. Using conservation farming the productivity of his land is four times that of other holdings in the area. Apart from vegetables he has also harvested a good quantity of maize. He has established such a good reputation that many buyers come to his place. His family no longer has to buy any vegetables and they help him with planting, watering, weeding and mulching. He too has planted trees and uses them both for timber and for firewood as well as to prevent erosion. Patrick came to be respected in his community and he found himself helping others. His training at MHAC enabled him to know when to plough, plant and cultivate his land and how to find markets; he was able to contribute to the United Nguva self-help group and to assist both his own family and his neighbours.

One of the most important factors in the development of MHAC has been the way it has won the approval both of the government and of sympathetic voluntary bodies. Secondly, management has been both efficient and indigenous with a high premium put on training and outreach. There has been no question of suggesting any holding is too small to profit from the new methods: there has also been encouragement for smallholders to work in co-operation with other producers. It is clear that these small-scale developments are bringing lasting sustainable benefit not only to one African country but to several of its neighbours as well.

MHAC is a beacon of light in a dark continent. When there is so much pressure on young people in the Third World to desert rural life for the magnet of the cities, it is showing that there is another much more satisfying way.

~ 17 ~
Comal
A Just Price in Honduras, Central America

COMAL is a cooking pot used in Honduras. It is also the name of the organisation which supports Cruz Grande Community Shop. Cruz Grande is just one of a network of hundreds of community shops spread all over the country of Honduras. It caters for a small community of just twenty families, well off the beaten track, up a steep muddy track leading from the tarmac road. The shop brings to those people the items which have been discovered to be the basic essentials for a household. Some such as fresh vegetables and freshly baked bread are produced on the spot: others like maize and rice have to be brought from another part of the country, as this is a coffee-growing area. There are one hundred and sixty items listed as the basic needs of the community. These include soap, sugar, vegetable fat, razors, tinned sardines, batteries, toothpaste, toilet rolls, matches and brooms. There is no need for the people of the village to look elsewhere for all their day to day wants, and they know that the goods will be of a high quality. They also know that they will be sold to them at a fair price: till the arrival of the community shop they were used to buying their goods at shops that aimed at getting as much profit as they could squeeze out of them.

Cruz Grande community shop is run by eleven partners, several of whom are related to each other. All work hard for the enterprise because it is theirs and they all have equal responsibility for its success or failure. The shop administrator is a twenty-seven-year-old single woman, Bautistina de Jesus Reyes Reyes. She has received training in bookkeeping from the Peasant Workers' Institute for Integral Learning and Training. She is responsible for ordering the goods from the regional warehouse in the nearby town of San Nicolas. Those collecting the goods walk to the town and then hire a vehicle to bring the goods back. If the road is impassable, as it can easily be in the rainy season, they have to carry everything on their backs. Although not all prices at the warehouses are cheaper than elsewhere, the overall cost is lower than getting goods from other sources. So they feel a responsibility to remain loyal to Comal so far as this is possible. Also they are able to sell their own produce: some of the members keep free-range chickens so that they can sell the eggs at the shop. This community shop not only benefits the local people by selling high quality goods at a fair price; it also engages in charitable work, for instance providing half the cost of medicines.

They have a vision for the future of their community. They hope to provide more employment by opening another shop as the people are spread out over a wide area. They hope to be able to offer low-interest loans and to help the smaller farmers by forming a coffee-growing co-operative.

In the last few years the farmers of Honduras have had to put up with floods, drought and one of the worst hurricanes in living memory, Hurricane Mitch which struck twice in 1998. In particular because of the hurricane there was an opportunity to give a new direction to the infrastructure supporting farming. Farmers all over the country were not only struggling with the effect of the hurricane and of the extremes of weather; they also suffered from problems endemic in nearly all poorer countries: there had been an inrush of imports favoured by devaluing the currency and the reduction in public spending brought about by structural adjustment.

Comal was a response to these conditions and it was the brainchild of a group of American Quakers. It brought together the work of twenty-four local organisations concerned with sustainable production and marketing. The basis of all its work is to see to it that both producers and consumers get a fair price for goods: their concern is not to make big profits but to improve the quality of life for all who participate in it.

Comal has one central warehouse near the capital city, but also regional warehouses covering fourteen out of the eighteen districts of Honduras; it has a particularly strong presence in the West of the country where there is the most poverty.

Comal does not only support shops. Many of its member organisations are in the business of growing crops. The Pozas Verdes Microenterprise brings together small farmers into a co-operative through which they get a fair price for their maize. It costs the growers just over £6 to produce two hundred pounds of maize and they receive £13.50, thus achieving more than one hundred per cent profit. Although farmers look after their own three-acre plots, all the land is owned co-operatively so that it cannot be sold by individuals.

In Pozas Verdes (meaning green ponds, good for bathing), the co-operative owns one hundred and eight acres for growing sugar cane and that land is farmed collectively. Fourteen out of the twenty-one households in Pozas Verdes are members of the co-operative – an average household has eight to ten people. Balbono Vasquez, the general secretary, also acts as a trainer with an organisation called the Peasant Workers' Institute for Integral Learning and Training, also known as ICFAI. This not only trains peasants in marketing techniques, but it also gives them a positive attitude to the land.

This is how he describes it:

> We like to promote an economy based on communities and solidarity; one that focuses on the relationship between human beings and nature. We have to look after our natural resources and know how to carry out sustainable agriculture and how to reforest our land. The economy is not just about money, but what we can do together as men, women and children in order to contribute to the benefit of the whole community: only that way can we develop. If we think about the economy and money, we all know that it goes to the rich and the powerful. The national economy doesn't benefit the poor, but just the few rich people and we teach people about that in our workshops.

The Microenterprise does not confine itself to farming, but like the Cruz Grande community shop it has been active in helping the local community to develop. Since it began in 1996 it has brought water and electricity to the village, not relying on central government to do these things, but using their own native wit and skills. They hope next to put in a telephone line and they would like to see Comal setting up its own sugar processing plant.

The treasurer of the Pozas Verdes Microenterprise, Alberto Polanco, said these words at a party given for donors who were visiting them:

Many people have asked us what the secret of our success is. We believe in sisterhood, brotherhood and fraternal love. And all of these motivate us. We maintain our unity and organisation. And we succeed because of our faith. We are very proud to say that no young people have ever left this town. No one has ever gone to the States, nor have they even moved to nearby towns or cities.

~18~
Rural Links
between India and Europe

IN 1981 three quarters of the people living in Natham, Tamil Nadu, a state of Southern India, had no land. In that year the Association for Sarva Seva Farms (ASSEFA) moved into the area and started its first project working with people who were on the margins of society.

Since that time ASSEFA has helped to set up village councils, village schools, youth clubs and women's forums. A People's Bank enables farmers to borrow on short-term credit for tools, machinery and seeds. Shops were established to sell local produce, and cottage industries were formed: these included units for the processing of rice and honey and for the extraction of essential oils. They also formed a co-operative for all the milk producers who wished to join. ASSEFA is a non-governmental voluntary organisation; it bases its thinking on Ghandian ideals of helping to bring about self-reliant rural communities imbued with a spirit of love, truth and justice. Throughout India there are plenty of such positive movements to set beside the growth of agribusiness on the one hand and the resultant landlessness on the other. But one of the things that makes this work in Tamil Nadu special is that it is part of a worldwide network called Rural Links.

At present Rural Links is bringing together similar projects in various parts of India, the West of Ireland, Albania, the Ukraine, Italy, Spain and West Devon in the UK. It is based on the belief that all countries have something worthwhile to share and that as we listen to each other so we can find new ways forward in our particular situations. Rural Links has identified certain ways in which this sharing may take place. One of these has been exchange visits: for instance Holsworthy Organics, a vegetable-growing co-operative in Devon recently made a tour of India studying similar projects there. This has been followed up by a visit to Devon by two women from India who manage projects specialising in small-scale agriculture and medicinal herb production and processing. A guide to sustainability is being produced which is based on the practice of partners' projects. It is available on the web and in hard copy and is being continually updated. It also looks for evidence beyond the initial core partners: Rural Links is working with non-governmental organisations in several European countries. For instance there has been collaboration with Italian and Spanish partners in promoting small-scale community enterprises set up and managed by women in the EU.

The partners that have clubbed together to get Rural Links off the ground are:

Action Village India, which is based in London and supports five rural development projects in India;

the **Association of Sarva Seva Farms**, mentioned above;

Crusade, which also works in rural Tamil Nadu creating self-help groups and health programmes;

the **Eco Club of Albania**;

Kerala Gandhi Smarak Nidhi, in South India;

Moy Valley Resources, based in County Mayo in the West of Ireland;

West Den International, Westden; and

the **Youth Environmental League of Prydniprovya** in the Ukraine.

The Albanian Eco Club was the brainchild of a group of scientists and journalists led by a Professor Ali Eltari: he is both a scientist and a writer as well as being an enthusiast for the natural world. The club has targeted young people and brings out a newspaper which is circulated free to schools and youth groups throughout the country. Because of its isolation Albania has retained a considerable amount of wild life that has been lost elsewhere in Europe. Besides four hundred wolves there are jackals, lynxes, wild boar, two kinds of wild cat and chamois. One of the challenges before the people of Albania is to ensure that, as the country becomes more open to foreign visitors, this precious heritage is not lost. Through Rural Links, representatives from Ireland, the UK and India have visited the country to help with environmental planning. In the other direction a farmers' co-operative from the North of the country has visited the UK.

The Irish Link is with the project Moy Valley Resources based in the north of County Mayo and the West of Sligo. The project has focused particularly on helping rural women to develop skills which will supplement their incomes. About twenty women are learning to use the bog wood which has emerged as a result of turf-cutting;

this they make into beautiful sculptures and crafts. In the words of one of the project managers, Ireland has suffered from the imposition of intensive farming by the EU and it will take years to rectify the effect this has had on the eco-system. Ireland shares this experience with many Third World countries, in particular India.

In Kerala, on the West Coast of India, Rural Links is working with the Kerala Gandhi Smarak Nidhi project helping small farmers to engage in what they call Balanced Farming. This enables agricultural workers who have only a small piece of land, say half an acre, to be immensely productive with that land by growing a rich variety of native crops. The workers are encouraged to grow a good variety of seasonal vegetables as well as other food crops like tapioca, yam and peanuts. One worker was helped to invest in a cow, ten chickens and a goat so that he now has his own fresh milk and eggs as well as plenty of dung on the garden. Both in Kerala and in Tamil Nadu a three-year project is under way to enable marginalised people to become more involved in decisions that affect their livelihoods.

Meanwhile the Link project in the Ukraine is coping with living in one of the most polluted countries in the world. Besides the continuing effects of Chernobyl, one of the Ukraine's main rivers has ten times more copper in it than is regarded as safe for health. As in Albania the project, which is called YELP, is concentrating on raising awareness, particularly among young people. It organises popular concerts, festivals and camps as well as conferences and seminars. YELP is working with the Devon Link and with the assistance of the British Council to produce a sustainability strategy for the whole country. A local group has developed a healthy, herb-based drink to provide an alternative to the omni-present Coca Cola.

In Devon itself there is a co-operative called The Proper Job producing organic food which it serves in its well-patronised café; this is also both a shop and a meeting place. Another initiative by the Proper Job is the recycling, reuse and repair of unwanted household items which are then sold on very cheaply. The co-operative is an active promoter of Local Exchange Trading Systems, a form of barter, and Local Agenda 21, which is concerned with local environmental projects for the twenty-first century. Westden International is now importing clothes and soft furnishings from India to sell in the UK and they have set up a new charity, Tamweed, which is concentrating on building links with an area of Tamil Nadu that was badly affected by the Tsunami.

One of the unexpected benefits of the horrors of the Foot and Mouth epidemic has been that the perception in some of the Third World of the state of farming in the UK has changed. Farmers from India visiting the UK at the time of the epidemic were shocked by what they saw. For too long there has been the belief that overdeveloped countries like the UK have everything to teach and nothing to learn from the underdeveloped countries. Both BSE and Foot and Mouth have demonstrated in a unique way that farming is as vulnerable in the UK as it is in less developed parts of the world. There is a gradual dawning that the Western industrialised brand of farming may not be the panacea that it was thought to be, say in the seventies. As local people are freed to come up with solutions that are appropriate for their own particular environment and to share those solutions across the world, so there can be renewed hope for small-scale growers, for organic farmers, even for the generally despised subsistence farmers. As the myth is dissolved that the only efficient farming requires massive inputs of machinery and sprays, so new buds can begin to appear without being nipped off in the interests of the wrong kind of globalisation.

~ 19 ~
Slow Food
Spreading Out from Italy
to the Rest of the World

CARLO PETRINI, the founder of the Slow Food movement, did not start his campaign with an office. He opened a restaurant. This was in the year 1980 and in the previous decade he had already been actively promoting his philosophy in two significant ways: he had founded a radical radio station which enabled him and his colleagues to make their views known throughout his region of Italy, and he set up a music festival encouraging musicians to play regional songs in people's homes.

His restaurant became the focus of people who wanted to enjoy good local food and wine in a relaxed atmosphere at reasonable prices. And so the first Slow Food Convivium was born. Slow Food uses the word Convivium for its local groups because it conveys the idea of enjoying life together. For one of the unusual achievements of the Slow Food movement is to combine a serious ecological concern with a great ability to savour the joy of consuming food and drink. Many ecologists are full of doom and many gourmets give little consideration to the state of the world, but Slow Food is for lovers of good food and wine who care very much about where the food they consume has come from and how it has been grown.

Since its beginning in Northern Italy the movement has grown to reach five continents and a hundred thousand people. The fundamental building block for Slow Food is the local Convivium. This may come into being anywhere where there is one person who is a member of the movement and is willing to get it going. Here is a sample six months' programme of a fairly typical Convivium in the UK:

In May there is a full day on a Saturday to make it possible for people of all ages to attend. Two Convivia have combined to make a visit to two neighbouring places of fine food production; one is an organic farm which breeds lambs and shorthorn cattle; the other is a maker of local cheeses. A coach has been arranged to make the visit that much more convivial. In the evening there is a dinner in an Italian restaurant where the chef is given a free hand to show off his skills.

The next event is a family picnic, again on a Saturday, to be held in the local botanical gardens. Following that the leaders of the Convivium have invited all members to their home to bring along food cooked according to recipes which people have inherited in their families. Then the botanical gardens is also the scene of a major wine-tasting and two months later tutored wine-tasting features in a Sicilian banquet held again in an Italian restaurant. And the programme finishes with a chance to savour Bangladeshi cooking.

But Convivia are only one building block of the movement. Slow Food uses another important Latin word to describe the next component. This is the Presidium, literally meaning a fortress. The aim of the Presidium is to help people throughout the world who are struggling to maintain the growing and marketing of endangered foods. Thus a small Alpine cheese-maker is given assistance to find his way through the EU Health and Safety directives. These are generally aimed more at large businesses but they can have a crushing effect on small ones. Presidia do not only give advice where appropriate; they use money from the central funds to support growers who are in financial difficulties. Slow Food receives its money from membership fees and, in some parts of Europe, corporate funding. For there are people both in corporations and in international organisations who recognise the value of what the Slow Food movement is achieving. For this reason it has been made a partner in the United Nations Food and Agriculture Organisation which is based in Italy. Slow Food also makes money on the sale of the Ark. This is a directory of foods worldwide which are under threat and which Slow Food is planning to save.

In the year 2000 a third building block was put in place and this was the creation of the Slow Food Awards. This has helped to shift the emphasis of the movement away from being mainly for the West to becoming a significant force in the Third World. To find award winners members seek out growers who have managed to rescue foods which were in danger of being pushed out by commercial interests. One classic example of this took place in the Rancho Grande in Mexico. Until recently the local cash crop had been coffee, but farmers were finding it increasingly difficult to make a living from this. So a young man called Raul Antonio Manuel persuaded the farmers to go over to growing vanilla, which had previously been grown in the area. This had the great advantage of requiring shade and being a companion plant, so that growing it has helped in the protection of forest trees. By 2004 five hundred farmers in twenty communities had clubbed together to grow and market this traditional food. And so Raul has become a Slow Food Award winner, which means that his work has been recognised internationally.

Another area where Slow Food has been very active is in education. Carlo Petrini has set up a University of Gastronomic Science at which people may graduate as Masters of Food. For this they need the ability to discern and appreciate the subtle flavours to be found in traditional food and drink. But Slow Food has also gained access to many schools, helping children to find a new sense of enjoyment of their food and also to grow their own food in school gardens. Two of the pioneer countries in this process have been Australia and the USA.

In the Western World Slow Food has developed the idea of creating Slow Cities where the hectic pace of life is gradually calmed down at every level. Many towns and cities in Italy have already signed up to this and the idea is spreading: Ludlow is one of the first in the UK. To those who say they are in too much of a rush Carlo Petrini replies that there has never been a time when many of us have had so much leisure – it's just what we do with that leisure time that crowds out the possibility of taking time over our food and drink.

Slow Food is both for town and country. One of Carlo's ambitions is that the rural areas should again become places in which it is 'beautiful to live' and that farmers should again have the time to be able to enjoy life instead of being bound to a wheel of greater and greater production.

It would be good if we could all take the time to stop and raise our glasses to the success of Carlo's ambition for the future of our planet.

~20~
What Can We Do?

THROUGHOUT this book the emphasis has been on the importance of eating food that has been produced locally. The obvious advantage of this is that it cuts down on the amount of miles that food has to travel. But it also helps the local economy and encourages local producers. Of course the ideal way of feeding ourselves locally is to grow our own food, but not everyone is in a position to do this, either through lack of time or through lack of access to land. Farmers' markets provide the next best source of locally produced food, though few people feel in a position to make all their food purchases at these. Another excellent source is veggie boxes and these raise the next vital issue: should we confine ourselves to eating only what has been organically grown?

It is widely believed that land which is organically farmed is much healthier than land which is fed largely by artificial fertilisers, and also, although some people in high places dispute this, that organic food is healthier for us. However we are often faced with a dilemma. Is it better to eat organic food that has travelled long distances to our plates or local food which has not been organically grown? There is no easy answer to this, for we have to weigh up the pollution caused by transporting organic food against the damage done by transporting and using the pesticides and fertilisers used in conventional farming. Of course the ideal is to buy food that is both organic and local wherever this is possible and the more we insist on both these qualities the more encouragement there will be to expand the local organic market.

If we do continue to buy exotic foods from far away, we then need to ask whether the people who have grown them are being paid enough for their labour and whether their living conditions are compatible with the demands of human dignity. It is now possible to find fair trade alternatives in many retail outlets for such items as bananas, chocolate, fruit juice, coffee and tea, but should we be asking whether we can manage without these luxuries which were unheard of in this country five hundred years ago? However, we also need to consider much more seriously than most of us do the need to pay fair prices for food produced in our own country.

There is another very important consideration when we are purchasing food that has its origin in animals. Are we prepared to take the trouble to check whether the meat, the fish, the dairy products and the eggs come from animals that have had a life worth living? Have the chickens whose flesh we eat and whose eggs we consume had the chance to scratch around in the earth or even to see the light of day? Have the pigs from which we have received our pork, our ham and our bacon been able to roam freely as pigs have always done, churning up the land as they go? Have the dairy cows been forced by the demands of profit margins to deliver more milk than is good for them and have the beef cows been free to graze when weather permits? Have the lambs been taken away from their mothers not out of necessity but because that is what suits the market? Have the fish been fed antibiotics against the lice that breed on them and kept in conditions that are totally against their nature? Not all fish farming is unnatural but salmon were never intended to be cooped up in small prisons. Are the fish we choose to eat endangered species or are there still plenty of them in our seas, lakes and rivers? It is not difficult to find the answers to at least some of these questions.

Local, organic, animal-friendly and fairly traded form the acronym LOAF. There is an organisation called Christian Ecology Link which is telling its members and anyone else who cares to listen to Use Their Loaf while shopping. But there are two serious obstacles to all this. Ever since we started importing food from our empire the people of Britain have become obsessed with the desire to buy food as cheaply as possible. For perhaps a quarter of the population buying cheap food may be a necessity, but for most of us it is a fad. After the Second World War we were on average spending one third of our income on food. Now it is down to one tenth. This means that we need only to spend one or two per cent more on improving the quality of our food to make a considerable difference for the producers.

The other obstacle is our desire for convenience. It is usually more convenient to buy all our food in one place rather than shop around; it is also usually more convenient to buy processed food rather than food that has to be cooked. This last deprives us of the opportunity of having fresh food on our table each day.

Each choice we make about what we eat and drink can make a world of difference. Every time we choose to spend our time, our energy and our money growing our own food in our garden or on an allotment, every time we buy direct from suppliers, whether through farmers' markets, farm shops, veggie boxes, WI markets, at a farm gate or a mill, every time we seek out and support an independent baker, butcher, greengrocer, fishmonger, grocer, general store, village shop, corner shop, market stall, co-operative or delicatessen, every time we buy food that is locally or organically produced, every time we go for meat of animals that have had a full and free life or else avoid eating meat altogether because of the way so many animals are treated, every time we stay or eat out or drink at a hotel, conference centre, retreat house, pub, guest house, bed-and-breakfast, cafe or restaurant that serves local food and drink, every time we cook and sit down to meals that have been lovingly prepared largely from fresh ingredients and take time both over the cooking and the eating, we are helping to make another world possible.

It has been predicted that at the present rate of consumption we shall have exhausted all known sources of cheap oil on which our global economy depends by the year 2015. This means that during the next ten years we need to support those structures that will enable us to switch from having mange-tout peas flown into the UK from Kenya to confining ourselves whenever possible to locally produced food. Local food will cease to be a food for the well-to-do: it will become a necessity for all but the well-to-do.

Appendix

RELEVANT ORGANISATIONS

Introduction
The Women's Institute, 104 New King's Road, London SW6 4LY; tel: 020-7731 5777
The National Trust, tel: 0870-4584000; www.nationaltrust.org.uk

Chapter 1
The Green Shop, 30 Bridge Street, Berwick-upon-Tweed TD15 1AQ; tel: 01289-305566; email: shop@thegreenshop.goplus.net
The Market Shop, 48 Bridge Street, Berwick-upon-Tweed TD15 1AQ; tel: 01289-307749; email: dave@samstone.fsnet.co.uk

Chapter 2
Graham Head, The Dovecot, Lowick, Berwick-upon-Tweed TD15 2QE; tel: 01289-388543; email: enquiries@piperfield.com; www.piperfield.com
National Farmers' Retail and Markets Association, PO Box 575, Southampton SO15 7BZ; tel: 01890-820338; www.farma.org.uk

Chapter 3
David Brettell, Charbagh, Lickar Moor, Berwick-upon-Tweed TD15 2TG; tel: 01289-388665, email: davidb@bordersorganicgardeners.org.uk; www.bordersorganicgardeners.org.uk
HDRA, The Organic Organisation, Ryton Organic Gardens, Coventry CV8 3LG; tel: 024-7630 3517; email: enquiry@hdra.org.uk; www.hdra.org.uk

Chapter 4
Denise Walton, Peelham, Foulden, Berwickshire TD15 1UG; tel: 01890-781328; email: info@BFRS.org.uk; www.bfrs.org.uk, www.peelham.co.uk

Chapter 5
Borders Machinery Ring Ltd, Galabank Mill, Wilderhaugh, Galashiels TD1 1PR; tel: 01896-758091, email: bmr@ringleader.co.uk; www.ringleader.co.uk

Chapter 6
Rural Regeneration Unit, Unit 5C, Lakeland Business Park, Cockermouth, Cumbria CA13 1QT; tel: 01900-606722; www.rru.org.uk
Countryside Alliance, www.countrysidealliance.org

Chapter 7
Heatherslaw Corn Mill, Ford Village, Cornhill-on-Tweed, Northumberland TD12 4TJ; tel: 01890-820338; email: tourism@ford-and-etal.co.uk
Washingpool Farm Shop and Restaurant, North Allington, Bridport, Dorset DT6 5HP; tel: 01308-459549; email: info@washingpool.co.uk; www.washingpool.co.uk

Chapter 8
Community Land Trusts, University of Salford, Room 214, Crescent House, The Crescent, Salford M5 4WT; tel: 0161-295 4454; www.communitylandtrust.org.uk
Community Farm Land Trusts, Hawthorn House, 1 Lansdown Lane, Stroud, Gloucestershire GL5 1BJ; tel: 0845-345 7599; email: cftl@communitylandtrust.org/farmland

Chapter 9
Daily Bread Co-operative Ltd, The Old Laundry, Bedford Road, Northampton NN4 7AD; tel: 01604-621531; email: northampton@dailybread.co.uk
Daily Bread Co-op (Cambridge) Ltd, Unit 3, Kilmaine Close, Cambridge CB4 2PH; tel: 01223-423177

Chapter 10
Jose Bove et al, *The World is Not for Sale*, published by Verso, 2001, ISBN 1859844057

Chapter 11
Association Avicole du Gers, Route d'Auch 32300, Mirande, France; email: contact@avigers.com; www.avigers.com

Chapter 12
Woodlands Farm, Kirton House, Kirton, Boston PE20 1JD; tel: 01205-722491; email: info@woodlandsfarm.co.uk

Chapter 13
Land Heritage, Summerhill Farm, Hittisleigh, Exeter EX6 6LP; tel: 01647-24511; email: enquiries@landheritage.org.uk; www.landheritage.org.uk

Chapter 14
The Green Patch, tel: 01536-481743; email: bldsanders@btinternet.com
Cultivating Communities (Community Supported Agriculture), Soil Association, www.cuco.org.uk

Chapter 15
Victorian Landcare, www.landcare.net.au

Relevant Organisations

Chapter 16
Manor House Agricultural Centre, Private Bag, Kitale, Kenya; tel 00-254-325-31151,email: mhac@net.2000.ke.com

Chapter 17
Christian Aid (which has helped to support Comal), 35 Lower Marsh, London SE1 7RL; tel: 020-7620 4444, email: info@christianaid.org.uk; www.christianaid.org.uk

Chapter 18
Rural Links, West Den International, Park Barn, Coryton, Devon EX20 4PG; tel: 0845-345 5077; email: osborne@westden.co.uk; www.rural-links.com

Chapter 19
Slow Food, Via Mendicità Istruita 8, 12042 Bra (Cuneo), Italy; tel: 0800-917 1232; email: slowinfo@slowfood.com, international@slowfood.com; www.slowfood.com; UK contact: Wendy Fogarty, wfogarty@compuserve.com

Chapter 20
Christian Ecology Link (contact: Laura Deacon), 3 Bond Street, Freehold, Lancaster LA1 3ER; tel: 01524-33858, email: info@christian-ecology.org.uk; www.christian-ecology.org.uk

Directory of local suppliers obtainable through local district councils or from www.bigbarn.co.uk

SOME MAGAZINES AND NEWSLETTERS

Country Living, National Magazine House, 72 Broadwick Street, London W1F 9EP; tel: 020-7439 5000; www.countryliving.co.uk

Country Smallholding, Argant Regional Ltd, Fair Oak Close, Exeter Airport Business Park, Clyst Honiton, Exeter EX3 2UL; tel: 01392-888475; email: editorial@countrysmallholding.com; www.countrysmallholding.com

Country Way, The Arthur Rank Centre, Stoneleigh Park, Warwickshire CV8 2LZ; tel: 024-7685 3073, email: katrina@rase.org.uk

The Countryman, Dalesman Publishing Group Ltd, Stable Courtyard, Broughton Hall, Skipton, North Yorkshire BD23 3AZ; tel: 01756-701381; email: editorial@thecountryman.co.uk

Countrywide Care (journal of Christian Rural Concern, editor David Swales), St Michael's House, 3 New Villa, Tavistock Road, Princeton, Devon PL20 6RW; tel 01822-890604

Earthmatters (magazine of Friends of the Earth), 26-28 Underwood Street, London N1 7JQ; tel: 020-7490 1555; email: info@foe.co.uk; www.foe.co.uk

Ecologist, Unit 18, Chelsea Wharf, 15 Lots Road, London SW10 0QJ; tel: 020-7351 3578, email: editorial@theecologist.org; www.theecologist.org. The magazine has a monthly survey of local and organic food.

Engage (newsletter of the Jubilee Centre), Jubilee House, 3 Hooper Street, Cambridge CB1 2NZ; tel: 01223-566319 email: info@jubilee-centre.org; www.jubilee-centre.org

Ethical Consumer, Ecra Publishing Ltd, Unit 21, 41 Old Birley Street, Manchester M15 5RF; tel: 0161-226 2929 (12 noon-6pm), email: mail@ethicalconsumer.org; www.ethicalconsumer.org

Good Housekeeping, National Magazine House, 72 Broadwick Street, London W1F 9EP; tel: 020-7439 5616; email: consumer.query@natmags.co.uk; www.natmags.co.uk

The Grocer, William Reed Publishing Ltd, Broadfield Park, Crawley, West Sussex RH11 9RT; tel: 01293-613400, email: grocer.editorial@william-reed.co.uk; www.foodanddrink.co.uk

Home and Family, The Mothers' Union, Mary Sumner House, 24 Tufton Street, London SW1P 3RB; tel: 020-7222 5533; email: mu@themothersunion.org; www.themothersunion.org

Kitchen Garden, 12 Orchard Lane, Wood Newton, Peterborough PE8 5EE; tel: 01780-470097; www.kitchengarden.co.uk

Magazines and Newsletters

Living Earth (newsletter of the Soil Association), Freepost, Bristol BS1 6ZY; tel: 0117-914 2447

Living Green (newsletter of the Lifestyle Movement), PO Box 2043, Bristol BS35 2WQ; www.lifestyle-movement.org.uk

The Marshwood Vale Magazine for West Dorset, Somerset and East Devon, Lower Atrim, Bridport, Dorset DT6 5PX; tel: 01308-423031; email: info@marshwoodvale.com; www.marshwoodvale.com

New Internationalist, 55 Rectory Road, Oxford OX4 1BW; tel: 01865-728181; email: ni@newint.org; www.newint.org

Organic Gardening, Sandvoe, North Roe, Shetland ZE2 9RY; tel: 01806-533319; email: organic.gardening@virgin.net

Organic Life, Guild of Master Craftsmen Publications Ltd, 166 High Street, Lewes, East Sussex BN7 1XU; tel: 01273-488005; www.thegmcgroup.com

Parish Pump (newsletter of the Conservation Foundation), 1 Kensington Gore, London SW7 2AR; tel: 020-7591 3111; email: info@conservationfoundation.co.uk; www.conservationfoundation.co.uk

Positive News, Positive News Publishing Ltd, 5 Bicton Enterprise Centre, Clun, Shropshire SY7 8NF; tel: 01588-640022; email: office@positivenews.org.uk; www.positivenews.org.uk

Prayer Guide for the Care of Creation (editor: Philip Clarkson Webb), 15 Valley View, Southborough, Tunbridge Wells TN4 0SY; email: opcwebb@tiscali.co.uk.

Resurgence, Ford House, Hartland, Bideford, Devon EX39 6EE; tel: 01237-441293; email: info@resurgence.org, www.resurgence.org

Smallholder, Hook House, Hook Road, Wimblington, March, Cambridgeshire PE15 0QL; tel: 01354-741538; email: liz.wright1@btconnect.com; www.smallholder. co.uk

Social Crediter (newsletter of the Social Credit Secretariat), PO Box 322, Silsden, Keighley, West Yorkshire BD20 0YE; tel: 01535-654230; email: socialcredit@FSBDial.co.uk

Third Way, St Peter's, Sumner Road, Harrow, Middlesex HA1 4BX; tel: 020-8423 8494, email: editor@thirdway.org.uk

Women's Health, Highbury Lifestyle, 1-3 Highbury Station Road, London N1 1SE; tel: 020-7226 2222

ALSO FROM SHEPHEARD-WALWYN

The Possibility of Progress
Mark Braund
'This is an impressive, important and readable book'   James Robertson

'... he is to be congratulated for opening up a debate based on the notion that we must radically rethink our economic system for it to be fair and sustainable'   John West, TRIBUNE

ISBN 0 85683 226 X   £14.95 pb

Globalisation for the Common Good
Kamran Mofid
'... a helpful and readable contribution to the whole debate about globalisation [that] challenges the view that "there is no alternative" and helps us think about what that alternative might look like'

Catholic Institute for International Relations

ISBN 0 85683 195 6   £12.95 pb

Promoting the Common Good
Bringing Economics and Theology Together Again
Marcus Braybrooke & Kamran Mofid
'I very much welcome this book and believe that its themes are of crucial importance to the world today'

From Foreword by Richard Harries, Bishop of Oxford

ISBN 0 85683 231 6   £9.95 pb

Lie of the Land
A Study in the Culture of Deception
Duncan Pickard

Subsidies, argues the author, a successful farmer, are the result of a tax regime that has crippled rural economies and village communities. Taxes encourage the sacking of employees in favour of capital-intensive methods. Subsidies enable large landowners to buy even more land thus extinguishing family farms. He proposes a tax reform that would reverse this trend.

ISBN 0 85683 227 8   £6.95 pb

For more information visit www.shepheard-walwyn.co.uk